THE SPIRITUAL PATH of AGING

Jo Ann Levitt

Copyright © 2023 by Jo Ann Levitt

The Spiritual Path of Aging

All rights reserved.
No part of this work may be used or reproduced, transmitted, stored, or used in any form or by any means graphic, electronic, or mechanical, including but not limited to photocopying, recording, scanning, digitizing, taping, Web distribution, information networks or information storage and retrieval systems, or in any manner whatsoever without prior written permission from the publisher.
In this world of digital information and rapidly-changing technology, some citations do not provide exact page numbers or credit the original source. We regret any errors, which are a result of the ease with which we consume information.

Cover Design by: Kristina Edstrom

An Imprint for GracePoint Publishing (www.GracePointPublishing.com)

GracePoint Matrix, LLC
624 S. Cascade Ave, Suite 201
Colorado Springs, CO 80903
www.GracePointMatrix.com
Email: Admin@GracePointMatrix.com

SAN # 991-6032

A Library of Congress Control Number has been requested and is pending.

ISBN: (Paperback) 978-1-961347-30-4
eISBN: 978-1-961347-31-1

Books may be purchased for educational, business, or sales promotional use.
For bulk order requests and price schedule contact:
Orders@GracePointPublishing.com

To Alice Hoffman-

Who had no idea
that she inspired me
to write this book.
Quite innocently,
she commented that
she'd be thrilled to
read a work based
on this very theme!

Thank you, Alice!

Contents

Introduction vii

Chapter One: Defining Your Spiritual Path 1

Chapter Two: Managing Loss 5

Chapter Three: The Art of Witnessing Experience 10

Chapter Four: Which Loss is the Hardest to Accept? 14

Chapter Five: Dealing with Ageism in This Culture 19

Chapter Six: Choosing Spiritual Practices Aligned with Your Path 24

Chapter Seven: On Love, Relationship, and Keeping Your Heart Open 31

Chapter Eight: The New Paradigm of Love 36

Chapter Nine: Transitions and Transformations 41

Chapter Ten: Managing "Old Age Loneliness" 45

Chapter Eleven: The Fierce Art of Letting Go 49

Chapter Twelve: Examining Beliefs about Aging 58

Chapter Thirteen: Tell a New Story 62

Chapter Fourteen: Enlightened Elders 69

Chapter Fifteen: What About Resilience? 74

Chapter Sixteen: A Cause for Celebration 77

Chapter Seventeen: What Is Your Chief Legacy? 81

Chapter Eighteen: Preparing to Die 84

Chapter Nineteen: A "Green" Departure 91

Chapter Twenty: Ready to Leave? 94

Appendix I: Exercises for the OLD-at-Heart 101

Appendix II: Time for Ritual and Prayer 105

Acknowledgments 117

Bibliography 121

Additional Resources 127

About the Author 129

Introduction

I have a question to ask you. Do you ever stop and think about the fact that you're getting older? Along with that—does it even occur to you that you're actually *aging*? I don't ask this to be funny, but rather to point out something that's not often on our radar. And that is—we're ALL getting older! But if you're like me, then one day you'll wake up with the stark realization of the aging process: O*h my God! I'm not a spring chicken anymore! I'm old!*

Most of us base our image of aging on various stereotypes, including gray hair, hunched-over-posture, wobbly walk, the use of canes or walkers, or the frighteningly slow word retrieval and brain processing that accompany aging. All along we've been witnessing parents, friends or relatives struggle with these issues, slowly losing their strength, solidity, or good sense, muttering about senior moments, or fading from active participation in life in the face of innumerable losses. One friend joked with me about her aging process, saying she couldn't understand why her teeth had turned yellow, while her hair was solid white. She added that it would have been so much easier if her hair had turned yellow, and her teeth had turned white!!

We think about aging largely as a process of moving from loss of memory to loss of mobility and morbidity issues to *moribundity* What we imagine (if we're not well along in years) is largely negative and uncomfortable. As a result, most of us keep postponing any sense of identification with or participation in this most difficult stage of life called aging. It's so much easier **not** to have to relate to your own mortality. Face it. Who me? I plan to live forever!

But there's an interesting moment, or series of moments, when suddenly we're faced with a dire event—an accident, a loss, or a shocking diagnosis—that sets us on a new path altogether. Suddenly aware of our fragility and vulnerability, we recognize we're finally sliding down the right side of the bell curve leading us into the ignominy of old age.

As a longtime spiritual teacher, guide, and counselor, I've spoken to a client who actually had this tender concern at the age of forty-nine—when she was about to hit the half-century mark of fifty. (*Yikes*, I thought to myself—*how will she feel when, like me, she's just a year away from eighty?*) But the awareness of transitions in life can hit anytime—whether we're turning sixty, seventy, or eighty (although by ninety, it's pretty much *old-hat*...).

As much as we're acquainted with the downside of aging, and plenty of reminders abound, including the physical limitations, changes in relationship, and the presence of loss—after a while, we can no longer deny we've entered life's closing chapter(s). At the same time, few of us grasp the real *up*side of the aging process. In spite of the decline and limitations, our later years offer us amazing new insights, perspectives on life, and opportunities, yes opportunities—for advancement along a whole new spectrum of growth and transformation. During this period, we have plentiful opportunities to grow in ways we might never have dreamed of before. It's not about improving our golf or tennis game. It's not about learning chess or traveling to Africa. What we can now claim is a certain expertise that very few under age sixty are ever privy to. That is the forging of a whole new spiritual path of aging.

> *The spiritual life can only be lived in the present moment, in the now. All the great religious traditions insist upon this simple but difficult truth. When we go rushing ahead into the future or*

Introduction

shrinking back into the past, we miss the [experience] of God, which can only touch us in the now.[1]

Spiritual process is hardly mentioned or elaborated for elders in our society. I love how different it is in India. Despite the emerging techno changes and materialism, there is still a deep understanding within Indian culture that life has different stages. After you've grown up, developed your career, or raised a family, it is understood that you are then free to investigate your spiritual nature. At sixty, it's not considered sacrilegious to forsake career and family to spend time in an ashram or pursuing religious studies And if you turn seventy-five, no one would question your right to leave everything behind and walk the path of a swami or *sannyasi,* sleeping in temples and filling your begging bowl through the good will of nearby villagers.

While we have no such customs built into the fabric of our society, still we have a *map* and can walk the pathway of our soul's own evolution. It comes through the act of aging itself; for, ironically, this very prickly time can offer up precious spiritual gems. That is, if we take notice. There are ways to shift our focus of attention so that we understand—at last! We've finally arrived at a point where we can glean wisdom, compassion, and equanimity from all we've said and done in the past seventy, eighty, or one-hundred years of life.

Some of my friends have asked how I came to write about this topic of spirituality and aging. Not that they doubted my so-called spiritual inclination, since I devised personal growth programs and taught more than twenty years at Kripalu Center in Stockbridge and also worked as therapist, teacher, and spiritual guide for more than twenty years at Canyon Ranch in Lenox—both places focused on health and healing. I am also deeply indebted to a group of congregants from the First Congregational Church in Stockbridge,

---

[1] Bourgeault (page 12)

who spent time with me reflecting on the characteristics of the aging process, which prepared the way for a revitalized spiritual path to emerge.

It's chiefly in the living of these seventy-nine plus years that I've come to identify the unique pathway available to us as we age. The offer is plainly in front of us to confront the loss and change along with the undeniable presence of ageism in this culture. Once we are able to witness everything that has been challenging or difficult, we are poised for the magic of transformation—where all that has been the source of pain or privation is now turned into grist for the spiritual mill of our awakening.

Later in this discussion we encounter the practice of witness consciousness, which is a variation on the well-known practice of mindfulness. In this context, it means engaging deeply with the spiritual injuries implicit in the aging process and applying deep powers of observation without blame or judgment. Then it points to softening and being fully present to the range of feelings, acknowledging and releasing the hurt, anger, or betrayal, to claim a kind of superior peace and neutrality. When I can look at the grave hurts and disappointments of my life with an appreciation for what they offer in terms of learning and self-knowledge, then I've entered a kind of "runway," taking off into the uncharted territory of spiritual awakening. And that leads me toward equanimity, acceptance, and—even further down the road—to what I like to call the experience of the *Enlightened Elder*. But trust me, if you choose this direction, you will need a walking stick, sturdy hiking boots (and possibly a machete), for this is no easy path. Still, it is here, beckoning to you. That is, if you recognize how old you are, and how much older you're becoming, and finally that there's no possibility of reversing this aging process, even if you subscribe to the eventual discovery of the fountain of youth.

Chapter One

Defining Your Spiritual Path

All of us follow some kind of spiritual path, whether we are aware of or care to acknowledge it or not. Essentially it serves as reinforcer and often transmitter of our core values and purpose in life. So if you're wondering what path you may be following, check in with your overall life mission and ask what actions have supported it all these years. Then go deeper. Consider what you came here to do in your time on Earth. Although reasons may differ, one or two themes generally emerge, such as, "I'm here to learn about love," or "I came to help others heal," or "I came to discover how to erect magnificent structures," or "I'm here to help grow sustainable foods for the planet," or "I'm here to guide people through their personal growth process."

Since science loves research and loves to go about proving what most of us already take for granted in relation to the aging process and your life purpose, it's evident that:

> *Having a purpose in life has been nominated consistently as an indicator of healthy aging... From a theoretical perspective, we find that endorsing a strong purpose in life continues to have meaningful reductions in the risk of dying...* [2]

Whatever your purpose may be, rest assured that it's firmly grounded in your heart's desire and your soul's capacity to manifest

---

[2] Hill and Turiano, pp. 1-2

multiple amazing experiences here on Earth. And speaking of "heart's desire," I love one of Jack Kornfield's messages in his recent book, *A Path with Heart*. Key teacher of meditation and mindfulness, quoting from the work of Carlos Castaneda, Kornfield assures us:

> *Any path is only a path. There's no affront to yourself or others in dropping a path if your heart tells you to do so... Study every path closely and deliberately; ultimately you must choose. But the only real question is—Does this path have **heart**?*[3]

As we begin our exploration into the combined experiences of aging and our choice of spiritual pathway, we'll take a deep dive into both areas. But first reflect on any paths you may have followed, left behind, or are just now considering as a possibility. These may be a combination of religious practice and affiliation, or identification with a physical activity, a practice, a community, or even communing with nature. Which path represents the real "path with heart" for you now?

It's always interesting to me, whether in my counseling practice or leading group work, to learn how people distinguish their religious paths from their spiritual paths—as if religion occupies one silo, spirituality occupies another, and *never the twain shall meet*. Of course, each does have its own defining characteristics. But whether you attune to the five calls for prayer in Islam, walk up to receive communion in church, *daven* to the rhythm of a Torah reading in synagogue, or practice yoga on your patio—you are still managing to accomplish what religion and spirituality hold in common, which is coming home to yourself—returning to a place of peace. That also means sensing or living into your connection with the Divine, and as I'll describe in greater detail in Chapter 3, creating the conditions for true witness consciousness to emerge. For our purposes now, witnessing is not just an act of observation—

---

[3] Kornfield (page 8)

it creates the impetus for an internal shift in consciousness that allows us to return to stillness, letting of pain or struggle.

Most people have heard the famous biblical passage from Psalm 46:10: *"Be still, and know that I am God."* Interestingly enough, many early definitions of spirituality incorporate the notion of stillness—not so much to recognize some external deity, but to be "brought inside oneself," or more commonly, to return to one's Source. Source can be called God. Source can be called Nature, and Source can be called the energetic Connection all souls share in common. Just as the source of a river is the origin from which the flow of water emanates, so too the Source within us gives rise to the flow of life and consciousness in each of us.

In a sense, then, any activity that calms the mind and restores our connection to Source can be deemed a spiritual endeavor. I like to think of a spiritual path as the overarching principle that may include aspects of one's religious background as well as many other things. It may be the daily walk in nature that sustains you, or serving in the soup kitchen, or visiting someone in your community who's homebound. In fact, there are *numerous* practices that serve the purpose of bringing us home to ourselves, as well as contributing to and generating new energy, new life, and new or amplified connections to Source. That may well be why the term *enlightened* reminds us that greater Light has entered our spiritual path. Light helps us see better; it warms us, and ultimately strengthens our access to the Divine, to inner peace, joy, and equilibrium.

Scrolling down the list that's included below, ask yourself which of the following activities are important (or even critical) to how you might define your spiritual path at this stage of life.

Regardless of the culture or tradition, invariably these qualities or conditions define a true Spiritual Path.

- Aligns with your core values and purpose in life.
- Involves the cultivation of wisdom and self-knowledge.

- Provides service to the community.
- Provides an inner sense of fulfillment and joy.
- Brings you into states of higher energy and vibration.
- Strengthens your connection to God, Spirit, or a Higher Power.
- May involve some type of practice, prayer, ritual, or reflection.
- Leads to freedom from suffering or pain.
- Becomes a deep expression of compassion and loving-kindness.
- Helps to light the way for others on their path.
- Aids in the release of old habits, ineffectual behaviors, or illusions.
- Creates the space for deep inner work and transformation.
- Offers a sense of lasting happiness and peace of mind.
- Leads ultimately to realization (referred to in some circles as the experience of enlightenment).

Given this variety of definitions, how might you characterize your own Spiritual Path of Aging? In what ways does it resemble your earlier versions of spirituality? In what ways is it a departure from the past, leading you to a whole new understanding and pursuit of your core spiritual values?

Chapter Two

Managing Loss

The biggest challenge that life presents us as we grow older is loss, which, in a certain way, is built into every segment of our life experience. However, there's a difference between the inevitable loss of one's childhood games and toys (which are generally replaced by more sophisticated digital games and toys as kids grow up) to the physical and mental losses that attend each stage of the aging process.

What can I do when I can't remember people's names? Or where I put things? All right, I didn't place my keys in the freezer; but still—it's awfully annoying when I keep misplacing them, along with my wallet, my glasses, and every other item that's fewer than ten inches in length! Is this the beginning of a far worse decline in memory and cognition that must be faced as I age?

A loss that sets us back can be a combined threat and source of grief—What if I fall? Oh, but I have fallen many times, and it scares me to death. Two years ago, I fell down the outside stairs leading to my second-floor apartment and caught myself with my left arm, thus breaking my wrist and dislocating my left shoulder. It all happened so suddenly; for one brief second, I was distracted by the sound of a leaf blower, and in the next instant I was lying face down in my driveway.

Losses come along in every stripe; some are noisy and some are silent. Most involve more than one set of capabilities; for instance, with my fall it was shaky motor skills coupled with sheer inattentiveness. I'm sure the same thing must have occurred across the street when an old man accidentally drove his car through the sheet glass window of the wine and cheese shop. Although he tried to stop, his reflexes were too slow and his foot on the accelerator too fast. There he sat, dazed and confused, unable to face the ensuing pandemonium when shop owners, police, and fire trucks arrived at the scene all at once.

Losses deepen. As we age, they seem to come together in more rapid sequence. The phone call came from Sanibel Island where my dear friends were vacationing several years ago. Paula was very ill; I could hear it in her voice. I prayed she and her husband would make it safely back to Massachusetts. But sadly, I never got to see my dear friend again, for she died of complications from cancer and an old surgery, not long after returning home.

The loss of others seems to mount day by day. It was more than a year ago that I mourned the loss of Mel Zuckerman, founder of all the Canyon Ranch facilities (in Tucson, Lenox, Las Vegas, and California). I had enjoyed his presence, sat through multiple engaging talks, gaining from his wisdom and his health triumphs through the years. It wasn't so long ago that a dedicated group of us gathered to honor his memory and listen to some of his fine stories while it rained heartily and we placed flowers at the site of what was now called the Mel and Enid Zuckerman pavilion at Canyon Ranch in Lenox.

Each death occurs like a sting or a gentle twist of the knife in one's heart. Some losses bring copious tears; others shut us down to friendship, connection, engagement, or places we loved to visit together.

No loss occurs as such a dire threat, however, as the gradual chipping away of our physical being, witnessing the decline in our mobility, our sanity, or our strength. What if you no longer have the strength to carry a heavy bag of laundry up the stairs? Or it's too frightening to get up on a ladder to change a light bulb or a smoke alarm? What if it's impossible to change the sheets on your queen-size bed, and your partner is no longer there to help you? Coupled with these multiple physical adjustments, which strip us of independence and the ability to care for ourselves unequivocally, we also suffer the simultaneous losses that we observe in our loved ones.

It pains me every time I visit my aging sister and observe her slow, difficult walk, trying to compensate for a prior botched knee replacement surgery and resulting injury to the sacrum and SI joint. Getting up from the table is painful for her; sitting back down is difficult; walking any distance is painful and managing to pull herself up a flight of steps is bewilderingly slow and hard. Seeing the look of agony on her face as she attempts to walk inevitably brings tears to my eyes, complicated by the fact that nothing seems to help, including my vain attempts offering Healing Touch and energy work. Then I think back to all her incredible activity—she, who loved to walk and run and who swam miles throughout the year. What unbearable frustration! What heartache!

Yet, the body has its own timeline for wearing out, which is often quite distinct from the timeline for our overall presence and participation in life as we know it. Nevertheless, all of this is hidden from those whose aging process moves very slowly and seems vaguely far off in the future. I could never understand my mother's fragility and refusal to walk long distances, until I myself had to have both hips replaced. There's nothing like the shock of pain and immobility to wake us up to the changes and concerns of aging.

It's amazing to me how blind young people are to the perils of aging. But of course, I include my earlier self in this analysis; I had no idea how different it would be when I "crossed the line" from youth into old age. Perhaps it's a godsend that we don't relate to the effects of aging until we ourselves grow old. But imagine for a moment that you could be part of an experiment. You're standing in front of a mirror—say, you're in the bathroom and it's first thing in the morning. You feel bright-eyed and bushy-tailed and have the good looks and broad smile of a thirty-something, or even a forty-something. While you're standing there, you witness an incredible change. In that very moment, your forehead wrinkles. Then crows' feet show up outside both your eyes and bluish-gray bags appear under both eyes. You watch in a combined reaction of fear, frustration, and fascination as age spots show up on your right cheek, while sun damage creates large reddish blotches on your left cheek. Several teeth are instantly gone, and you're surprised at the number of implants you find where those teeth used to be. Your jawline sags and as you gaze downward, you're shocked to see not one but two or three double chins and a kind of goose flesh hanging there on your sagging neckline. It's overwhelming. But the experiment's now complete. (And lucky for you, your face resumes its youthful appearance!)

Now in real life we are saved from such a precipitous event as the one I've just described. The line of demarcation may still be miles away for that person in front of the mirror. As yet, there is hardly a whisper or a clue to the fact that they're aging. And who knows when the first acknowledgment of aging will set in—after the lines across the forehead show up or the creepy double chin? This aging process is distinct and difficult, and places those of us who've managed to come through our sixties, seventies, eighties, or even our nineties into a whole different class of citizenship—almost as if we're foreigners or have landed here from some other planet. For me personally, the hardest thing to face is the gradual disappearing act that I experience. As an aging person I'm just not seen or noticed, and sometimes I really feel invisible—to myself as well as to the world at large.

Yet we're all a product of our culture. It wasn't so very long ago that I felt prejudiced against the weakness I perceived in elders. I would see an old man walking down the street with his head facing downward and his back curved like a *C*, and immediately I'd want to shout at him, "Straighten up! Try to walk upright!!" But that prejudice entails forgetfulness or just plain ignorance of the prior issues that brought him to that stage of infirmity. The judgment I held in regard to his situation was no different than the judgment I held around my mother's immobility in her later years. Clearly, he could do better. Clearly, she could have done better. We can all do better (thinks little Miss Perfection)—if only we make the effort! If only we take control! At heart, it's the same kind of prejudice that wants to make fat people thin or homeless folks get a job or couch potatoes get off their butts; DO something. Take action! Don't be such a wimp! And this is at the heart of prejudice: we see the end result without reckoning with the various conditions that mounted together one-by-one to bring about this inevitable state of decline.

Judgment doesn't help. Criticism doesn't help. But oh, how hard it is to observe weakness or failings—whether in ourselves or in other people. As Thich Nhat Hanh used to say, "Seeing and loving go together. Great understanding gives rise to great compassion."[4] And somehow the aging process helps us turn that corner. When faced with the inevitable losses, illness, and changes that aging brings about, we have a little more understanding, and possibly—just possibly—the ability to experience compassion. For this old person is not someone else holding a cane or limping down the street now, but our very own selves that we are coming to terms with as we face the prospects of old age.

---

[4] Hanh (Page 6)

Chapter Three

The Art of Witnessing Experience

If we are staking our future in actually pursuing a spiritual path, we must begin to seek a new direction. Much of this has to do with the distinct way in which we pay attention to our experience. The truth is that most of us could use an upgrade to our awareness as we move through life. In order to break out of autopilot, we need to engage more deeply, and become more consciously attuned to experience. We must be willing to stop and take notice. The practice of *witness consciousness* invites us to be present with and for ourselves as we are—with an attitude of openness, kindness, and generosity.

> *Now is always the right time—because it is the only time! Whatever you're experiencing in this moment is perfect exactly as it is. It is your special 'curriculum' of the present—of life unfolding here and now. By practicing mindfulness, you are cultivating extravagant welcome—unflinchingly welcoming in whatever arises in the mind.*[5]

Imagine you're attending a trial and you have a chance to observe the ideal witness. That person is called to take the stand in some kind of criminal proceeding. Why is she considered the ideal witness? That has to do with the fact that she saw the event as it took place; she carefully observed the participants, the action, and the outcome, and when she was called to the stand, she was able to

---

[5] Jon Kabat Zinn, page 115

report out every detail without taking sides! Strange as it may seem, that last condition places her in the ideal category, creating the template for what we ourselves hope to accomplish as we develop witness consciousness. The practice of witness consciousness involves paying attention to experiences without taking sides or rejecting difficulties. When we're no longer fighting against things we don't like or craving experiences we do like, we're preparing the ground for expanded tolerance and the ability to *witness* life with compassion and neutrality.

We engage the witness by first becoming aware that we're struggling or having intense reactions. This awareness comes as attention without tension, an ability to be conscious of thoughts and feelings generated without getting caught in their negative emotional states. Otherwise, we're drawn right back into the struggle. When the mind is disciplined enough to enter witness consciousness, then awareness works as a self-corrective mechanism.

> *Accessing witness consciousness is an incredibly powerful development. Nevertheless, with the witness, there can still be a strong sense of dualism. Noticing my rib cage expanding and contracting as I breathe, I am witnessing this experience. It feels relatively present and vital because I'm here and I can feel what's going on. I'm breathing in; I'm breathing out. However, there's a sense that a "me" or an "I" (sometimes called the watcher) is observing something. There's a subject and an object being observed. However, as our attention stabilizes further and our awareness deepens, we gradually move beyond that, relaxing the sense of a separate observer and beginning to dissolve the subject-object duality, so as to move into direct, non-dual experience, and even further—into pure presence, pure beingness.* [6]

---

[6] Fleet Maull Ph.D. (E-book online)

Witnessing is the most skillful means to face reality for it entails getting ourselves out of the way and bypassing the conditioning of the mind. We do this by becoming so fully engaged—both in the outer and inner worlds of experience—that whatever presents itself, whether physical sensation, vision, feeling, thought or movement of energy is worthy of our full attention. By allowing all feelings and suppressing nothing, we open the door for the full range of sensations to appear. In that way nothing is hidden or pushed away.

Moving into the heart of feelings and sensations in this way was often referred to as "Riding the Wave" at Kripalu Center. In our early programs we had created a simplified protocol, called BRFWA, which stood for "breathe, relax, feel, watch, and allow." But the feeling part can often be the most difficult. Getting to the heart of deeply held hurts, rage, or sadness is often a bumpy ride. We'd rather just stay on the surface. However, if we dive in, we can bear the intensity of feeling, knowing full well that the wave will eventually bring us back to shore. This is aligned with the idea that emotion is actually *E-Motion,* or energy in motion. It is asking to move, shift, change, or morph into something else entirely. Being present to such deep emotions helps clear the mind and free up the resultant static within our energy fields. Emptying our minds, we then embrace a greater reality, because the witness can see the mind *interacting* with itself. If we can see how we interact with thoughts and feelings, we no longer have a need to identify so deeply with them.

Mindfulness thus enhances our capacity to witness. Through witnessing, we discover the role we play in distorting or fighting with experience. When we stop struggling, we no longer divide our attention and, as a result, we no longer divide or deplete our energy. Being present without trying to alter what's happening helps us abide in calmness—our natural state of being. Witness consciousness is the gift that allows us to be unconditionally present for life as it is.

The Art of Witnessing Experience

When we perceive things as they are, a light develops out of events that often points us in the right direction or leads to new outcomes. Being mindful is not a substitute for participating fully in life or for changing things we hope to change. On the contrary, it provides a springboard from which authentic action can arise.

In truth, any therapist worthy of their name provides the space and permission for this consciousness to be activated and fully experienced. It may be referred to in different ways, such as holding space, allowing feelings to surface, being mindful, bearing witness, or reflecting back what's truly going on. Essentially, it's the same thing that we strive to develop within ourselves when we stop fighting, judging, or denying our core experience, and that is what we call *witness consciousness*.

> *The deep knowing that is wisdom arises through the simple act of giving someone or something your full attention. Attention is primordial intelligence, consciousness itself. It dissolves the barriers created by conceptual thought... [and] [j]oins the perceiver and the perceived in a unifying field of awareness.*[7]

Giving something our full attention can mean so many different things. For me, the most important aspect has to do with fully living the experience—being willing to be present to whatever emotions surface, and along with that, whatever pain is there to be experienced. It's not so much an orientation to what brings you down or conversely what lifts you up; it's what has arisen here and now, period. As we practiced and taught at Kripalu Center; however, several of us long-term program directors soon tired of the seriousness and potential self-absorption arising from so much *self*-study. As a result, we delighted in making fun of each other and were cautioned in turn against applying too much "witless consciousness."

---

[7] Tolle- (Quote from *Basic Delusion*)

Chapter Four

Which Loss is Hardest to Accept?

> *When the fundamental nature of things is not recognized, the mind's essential peace is disturbed to no avail. The Way is perfect as vast space is perfect, where nothing is lacking and nothing is in excess. ... Do not seek for the truth; Only cease to cherish opinions.* [8]

As we age, the catalogue of losses becomes endless. And yet our spiritual task includes learning to be present and to release the charge beneath these difficult events, so that we come back if not to full freedom and joy, at least to a sense of acceptance or neutrality. Below are a series of thoughts gathered from friends, clients, church members and co-workers, acknowledging many of the losses experienced across the spectrum of our aging process.

- If I sit down, there's no guarantee I'll be able to get back up again. I've lost all the strength in my legs.
- I've lost my beautiful home; it was just too much space and too much for us to handle, once the kids moved out.
- I've lost a sense of direction with my failing eyesight; I don't trust myself to drive anymore.
- I've lost touch with two of my three children. My grown son keeps in touch sporadically, but both my daughters are on

---

[8] Clarke, ed. (page 1)

- their own. It's clear they don't need help or advice from their mother. In fact, they don't even want me around.
- I've lost two-thirds of my savings, through poor investment strategies, exorbitant health bills, and my own stupidity, giving away money to too many good causes, so that now I'm kind of in the *lost cause* category myself.
- With one knee and two hip replacement surgeries, I've lost the ability to walk any distance and find myself relying on my pain medication too much. For all intents and purposes, I'm addicted.
- I hum along now when I go to a concert because I can no longer sing. I used to sing professionally as a soprano but now my voice is useless. I can't tell you how painful it is to not to be able to sing those beautiful arias.
- I've lost interest in social media. I hardly ever text, but I do email, and I wish my grandchildren would respond. It's almost as if I've written to them from New Zealand; that's how long it takes to ever get a response back from them. But of course, they don't live in New Zealand; they live three blocks away in New Jersey.
- I'm glad there are nurses and aides around this assisted living place I've just moved into; however, I'm scared because lately I've been having dizzy spells, and twice I passed out. Even the doctors are puzzled and don't know what to do with me…
- No one knows what it's like to have neuropathy. Yes, they gave me physical therapy for my surgery; yes, they helped me (a little) with two spinal fusions, but even the doctors shrug their shoulders when you tell them you have neuropathy in both feet and any attempt at walking is painful.
- I feel really stupid telling people that I'm grieving the loss of my sweet cat Joey, but it's true. He meant the world to me. He was all I had to live for.

We could go on and on with this list, for indeed the series of concerns and complaints is endless. And we sense that their presence is mounting as we age; our faculties slow down or give way, and we have some acute or anxious feelings about losing control. Little by little things are falling away; it's not our game anymore. It's someone else's. The most difficult part is that no one really understands the pain we're experiencing or the grieving process that we're going through. In most cases, great pain or loss are just not subjects for polite conversation.

In her seminal work, *It's OK That You're NOT OK*, Megan Devine sheds new light on the cultural environment that belittles or tries to "fix" the pain of grief or loss. She tells it like it is on the very first page of her lengthy discourse:

> *You don't need solutions. You don't need to move on from your grief. You need someone to see your grief, to acknowledge it... [and] to hold your hands while you stand there in blinking horror, staring at the hole that was your life.*[9]

Although no one wants to approach end-times with a severe or critical diagnosis, such as cancer or cardiovascular disease, still as we age many of us must learn to grieve, make adaptations, or get help staring at that hole... given sudden obstacles that obstruct our path. But nothing helps if we're urged to just "move through it." Likewise, many other losses must take the time that they take for us to grieve and experience them, and if at all possible—move on. Twice I personally experienced the kind of loss that doesn't easily retreat or go away. I've dubbed it with a new title, referring to it now as *Losing Place; Losing Face*.

As I mentioned earlier, I was a long-term teacher, counselor, and disciple at Kripalu Center, both in Pennsylvania and later in Massachusetts, where we developed our highly sought-after Center

---

[9] Devine (page 3)

Which Loss is Hardest to Accept?

for Yoga and Health. Arriving on staff as early as 1974, I was a member of the first group to help create a health center in Pennsylvania, and in 1982 I moved to Stockbridge to help develop new personal growth programs, such as Self Esteem, Quest for the Limitless You, and more. After multiple regime changes, Kripalu finally sent me on my way (delicately) in the early oughts of this century. Though I had my wits about me and was likely a better teacher at that point than twenty years prior, still the message was clear. They wanted a younger, slimmer, prettier version of me to grace their program rooms—with the emphasis on *younger*.

It is a very subtle, covert operation that takes place all the time and in every setting. While seeing clients at Canyon Ranch in Lenox, there was unmistakable evidence of its presence there for me, too. Three years ago I suffered a great loss when we witnessed yet another regime change. Mel and Enid Zuckerman had retired altogether from managing the various resorts, and so a new CEO took up his position in Fort Worth, Texas and hired his cohort, who gathered data, compared statistics, and crunched numbers beautyfully to create the new performance-oriented Canyon Ranch.

Now, please understand: Performance is very important in terms of sports, athletic endeavors, or even managing certain health conditions. However, I was a counselor and guide in the department known as Spiritual Wellness. If we start turning spiritual practice into a "performance," we tend to lose the meaning of a true spiritual endeavor. Why would you take such a sacred part of life and view it through the lens of *performance*? It turns it into some kind of competition or spectator sport that frankly never made sense to me. At any rate, I was soon to be divested of this opportunity altogether.

Although I have an RN degree, a master's in education, and a degree in Healing Touch, I was deemed no longer qualified to lead Soul Journeys, the very same service that I had designed and introduced to the Ranch some twenty years earlier. It was an enormous blow to me. I learned that the incoming management had developed new credentials for what I had been doing all during my tenure there. At that point, in order to lead Soul Journeys, I would need a Master of Divinity degree. (Although, in truth, there is no license or qualifying degree for leading shamanic work or Soul Journeys.) If it hadn't reduced my income so drastically that I had to seek outside employment to survive, I might not have been so upset or distraught.

But then Canyon Ranch ended any remaining concerns I might have had by dropping me out of the Spiritual Wellness Department altogether, because I wasn't able to keep up sufficient hours. Needless to say, no one questioned why I had to look for an outside job after so many years of service at Canyon Ranch. The answer was simple; I was no longer able to make ends meet, and our guest registrations were simultaneously dropping.

Sometimes the loss occurs as a slap across the face, but more often it lands as an excision of the fibers of one's heart and soul. What happened for me at Canyon Ranch occurred as a brutal loss of work, engagement, and belonging with simultaneous denial of the amazing work I had offered over the course of twenty-three years. But what was hardest to bear was the fact that management was completely unyielding. After all my years of service, they had no interest in hearing my point of view, taking care of me, or creating a sustainable plan for the future. Amid all the losses sustained, I have to say that their callousness hurt me more than anything else.

Chapter Five

Dealing with Ageism in This Culture

A new paradigm for understanding the aging society is necessary in the face of a rapidly expanding population of older adults. Ageism is a very serious issue. While it can theoretically be directed toward any age group, the vast majority of studies focus on older adults. Learning more about its effects can be a key foundational resource for older adults. Research studies carried out in the past 15-20 years increasingly point to ageism (or age discrimination) as a risk factor associated with increased stress, anxiety, depression, and lowered life satisfaction for the elder population.[10]

While gathering data for this important subject of ageism, I was greatly surprised to find that in terms of worldwide policy, work with ageism has hardly begun to come of *age*. For example, back in 1948, the United Nations General Assembly adopted a Universal Declaration of Human Rights, emphasizing the fact that all individuals have the same rights: "without distinction of any kind, such as race, colour, sex, language, religion, political or other opinion, national or social origin, property, birth or other status." Yet, nearly eight decades later, age is still not an *explicit* part of that UN declaration.[11]

---

[10] Kim and Kang (page 88)
[11] Ibid (page 89)

The Spiritual Path of Aging

Likewise, if you go onto the United Church of Christ website, arguably one of the more liberal-minded of mainstream churches, you will find even today that their banners list all the reasons that discrimination is unacceptable (including race, religion, skin color, gender) *except* for aging.[12] How interesting! You'll meet up with discrimination based on the color of your skin, your ethnic origins, your sexual orientation, or gender fluidity, but little did you know that as you age, there's another "kick in the pants" to look forward to—you'll be ignored because you're old. In many cases, aging is an invisible act. Of course, it doesn't take a great stretch of imagination to recognize how biased we are in this culture towards youth, beauty, and life before Medicare. Dozens of research studies confirm the fact that ageism is alive and well, while we—*the recipients*—are actually on the path to death and dying.

The funny thing about this invisibility business is that it's subtle and very hard to explain if you haven't directly experienced it. But in a flash, my experience last Halloween in Stockbridge popped into my mind. I wasn't sure why it had, but I remembered how much fun I had had making my funny clown costume, replete with a mask that I painted myself—with a big red nose. I hadn't realized that the get-up was intimidating to kids though. When I approached the parade on Main Street, I noticed some children shunning me or running to grab onto their parents. I was surprised and a little sad, for I had hoped to have the opposite effect. But then, all of a sudden, a little three-year-old-boy named Jack showed up with his parents in tow. His costume was spectacular: He was dressed as a UPS truck driver with a nicely painted little truck perched on his shoulders. He seemed to have no fear or suspicions about me, and all at once, he reached his tiny hand out in my direction and held it out there for me to grab hold. I looked to his parents for permission, and when they nodded their heads and Jack's hand was firmly in mine, I felt joy beyond compare. Jack and I wound up marching the

---

[12] United Church of Christ website

whole length of Main Street hand-in-hand (while his folks carried the homemade truck that had slid off his shoulders).

In some ways that experience was eerie; but in pondering it again, I understood that Jack actually *saw* me! He saw beyond the mask and the costume and felt completely comfortable in my presence. The reason this event popped up in my mind must be obvious—it has to do with the notion of seeing *beyond the mask*. I realize that it's not easy for younger folk to see the real person behind the age spots, the crinkly face, or the saggy breasts. We look so *old*—how can we still be alive? What Jack taught me, however, was that we all have an energetic connection with one another that totally supersedes appearances. It's just that we lose track of that connection. But what a moment of complete exhilaration when it is restored!

So much research—so many frightening statistics. Did you know that gray hair is an inevitable by-product of aging? I found it fascinating that the Library of Congress has actually documented that the chances of your hair graying increase 10-20 percent every decade after the age of thirty. So lookout! There's also studies affirming the point when we've "crossed the line" between middle and old age. It made me laugh when someone depicted that "line" as obvious. You'll know you've crossed over when younger people make fun of what you're wearing. "Why, those are old ladies' clothes!" Or you've crossed over if you only love music from 1960 or 1970 or have a thing about keeping old china and tea sets at hand. My favorite qualification; however, is if you react to anyone treading on your lawn![13]

Now, I don't have a lawn, and I don't have much in the way of good china or tea sets. Still, it seems as if there is a line of demarcation, and it may not be just between younger and older folks. It probably exists between *all of us* no matter what age we are! Perhaps what

---

[13] *Ten Signs* (Online Article)

happens is that as we age, we find it hard to relate to anyone who's more than twenty years older than we are. I know it's a strange hypothesis, but consider those whom you feel free to look at or study as you're walking down the street and those whom you choose to ignore. Chances are more than likely that your focus leans towards youth.

Even among those of us who face different stages of the aging process, there's still plenty of ageism to track. It both pains and amuses me when I receive my new issue of *Focus on Healthy Aging*, and the ad accompanying the newsletter touts some kind of positive reminder, such as: "Losing your Keys? Forgetting People's Names? Not sure why you wound up in the Kitchen? Not to Worry! *These are signs of normal aging*"(italics mine).[14] It's the use of "normal aging" which either distresses me or makes me laugh, depending on my mood (and also whether it's a loss of keys disturbing me in that moment—or something more dire, such as accidentally banging my head on the cabinet door—and simultaneously forgetting why I came into the kitchen)!

Please tell me: For god's sake, what is normal about the aging process? Is it your dry alligator skin that feels like it will peel off at the slightest provocation? How about the complete loss of muscle mass—such that the flab hanging down from my arms looks more like pizza dough waiting to be rolled out and baked than it does arms or skin? Or is it my clumsiness and balance issues, perpetually dropping things or bumping into walls? Or is it forgetting to call my brother or keep an important appointment? Or some difficult illness that can't seem to be diagnosed but leads inexorably to decline? I find "normal" to be an abnormally *ageist* adjective. Again, look around. Everything in this culture is pretty well lined up to "normalize" aging, which essentially translates as finding ways to minimize aging. That's because none of us wants to admit

---

[14] *Focus on Healthy Aging*-Newsletter

Dealing with Ageism in This Culture

it's where we'll all wind up. In fact, the most distressing of all reactions is the attempt to disappear us old folks from view altogether.

Now, I'm not referring to some nefarious political cleansing scheme getting rid of the elder population. No, I'm talking about a popular game that's played everywhere in this country. It's called *Let's Make Believe.* And the rules of the game are simple: Let's make believe that old people don't exist. Pass by that old lady and don't dare look up from your phone to say hello. See that old man pushing that walker around in the supermarket? Oh, of course, I forgot; you can't really see him because, in fact, he doesn't exist. It's this ubiquitous issue of being rendered invisible that is so difficult for us to acknowledge and even more difficult to deal with.

Sometimes I want to weep at my own invisibility. Sometimes in an angrier frame of mind, I want to stop someone on the street, and yell, "Look at me please! Don't look away. Don't pretend I'm not here just because I'm old and I have gray hairs on my chin and age spots on my hands! I'm still here, and I am not a figment of my imagination or yours. See!" Then, like that pivotal moment in the Gospels when Jesus calls Doubting Thomas forward so he can test whether this *revived* Jesus is authentically real, I suddenly grasp how I'll copy that event. I'll make that person who's avoiding me come up real close, and then I'll push their fingers into the deep wound of my aging process.

But when I come out of my stupor and am back in my living room, reading that newsletter, I'm reminded once again that I can certainly "Live Longer and Healthier by Walking More."[15]

---

[15]*Focus on Healthy Aging*-Newsletter

Chapter Six

Choosing Spiritual Practices Aligned with Your Path

In his beautiful book, *A Path with Heart,* Jack Kornfield guides the reader through discussion and ample support for discerning a spiritual path that provides greater meaning and purpose for each stage of life. Just as we continue moving through different cycles of life, our spiritual practice must also evolve and be aligned with the accompanying shifts in our life experience. What can support our new direction may be letting go of our habit of compartmentalizing everything in life, as Kornfield points out so powerfully.

> The walls of our compartments are made of fears and habits, of ideas we have about what should or shouldn't be, of what is spiritual and what is not…We fear the personal because it has touched us and wounded us most deeply, and this is what we must examine to understand these compartments. Only when we have become aware of these walls in our own hearts can we develop a spiritual practice that opens us to all of life.[16]

Our lives are constantly undergoing change. Of course we frequently become aware of this along the continuum of existence, but it seems more poignant and less controvertible as we age. This issue of aging may frequently involve separation, dismissal, or

---

[16] Jack Kornfield: A Path with Heart (page 190)

Choosing Spiritual Practices Aligned with Your Path

invisibility. However, the most important thing is that we not become invisible to ourselves—and that we not discount our accumulated wisdom, know-how, or understanding just because our faces are wrinkled or our gait has slowed down. Life changes. All the compassion and understanding we hope to receive from others must now become the gift that our souls entrust to us. It is we who are called to develop meaningful relationships here on Earth, and that can only evolve through connection with ourselves, and a deep dive into whatever we cultivate as our authentic Spiritual Path of Aging.

In her work, *It's OK That You're Not OK*, Megan Devine speaks about the purpose of spiritual practices, taking a broad look at some of the cultural conditioning that we must learn to "uncondition" or let go of within ourselves:

> *Spiritual practices in any tradition… are meant to help you live what is yours to live, not make you rise above it. These tools are meant to help you feel companioned… to give you a tiny bit of breathing room. That's not the same thing as making your pain go away. Rather than help us rise above being human, teachings in any true tradition help us become more human.*[17]

The time comes to ask yourself, "What value does a spiritual path hold for me?" Given all the shifts and transformations of the aging process, there may be something about this stage of life that inclines us more in the direction of spiritual practice. So how committed are you to discerning what might work for you? Even as our focus gradually begins to shift, there's still everyday work to do; there's adult children visiting or living nearby; there's volunteering, not to mention having dinner at the club, movies with friends, or the endless pursuit of filling time for the sake of filling time—something many of us good doers understand implicitly. However, the quality that distinguishes spiritual practice from other

---

[17] Devine (page 50)

endeavors is the willingness, in a sense, to step out of linear time as we know it. *Oh dear*, you may be thinking. *Does that mean I must sacrifice my morning coffee to sit for meditation?* (Surely practice would evaporate if it were perceived as a trade-off for caffeine!) Yet life frequently offers multiple routines and activities that distract us from a deeper search.

For me, resorting to spiritual practice is an absolute necessity and a *sine qua non*—that is, nothing can replace it for me when I'm craving peace of mind, relief from internal struggles, or external conditions, such as the mere fact of having landed here on Earth. I am eternally grateful for all my religious and spiritual affiliations—especially life in the ashram—for whatever it may have produced in the way of interpersonal conflict, it certainly created an environment in which practice was foundational. It still amazes me remembering how a small group of us woke up early every morning and were out jogging down the road by 4 a.m.! Then we gathered in the meditation room and did yoga postures, followed by pranayama (breath-work), and finally entered into deep states of meditation and calm. Even today that kind of practice stays with me, although I admit I am no longer out jogging at four o'clock in the morning.

Now my practice is more focused on gathering my energies into a place of peace and internal concentration. Besides movement and asana, I also resort to mantra chanting, prayer, and occasional toning—which is the use of wordless sound to center and move into deeper states of meditation. I am very grateful for the fact that long practice has conditioned my mind and body for continuing long practice. Each day's practice reinforces getting up the following day, and is invariably accompanied by a strong intention to be balanced and at ease before I head out to work in the morning.

Unless there's a serious craving for the kind of peace and grounding that inner immersion brings to us, there's not much hope for developing a practice. Usually, the first and most critical variable

Choosing Spiritual Practices Aligned with Your Path

has to do with one's intention. How much do you desire the effects of a true practice? This can't be stressed enough. Desire and intention are totally interwoven and affect your participation from the get-go.

It's like an old story that comes to us from India. There we find a young man seeking counsel from a great wisdom teacher in the state of Gujarat. Although he approaches the teacher many times, begging for an audience, it isn't until the teacher takes him out into the middle of the Narmada River that the real teaching begins. The teacher repeatedly asks the young man how much he wants to study with him, and the young man repeats the same thing back, "Why very much, of course! Why do you keep asking me?" Then suddenly this old wise man grabs him and holds him under water until he's choking, sputtering, and coughing up water. "What a mean thing to do!" he yells, once he pops back to the surface. And in that moment he receives this advice, "When it's as critical for you to receive spiritual knowledge as it is to take your very next breath, then call me. We'll begin in earnest."

So what will help you "breathe again"? Is there a particular intention that drives your choices? And are you willing to "stop time" in order to take up a practice—which in effect means setting time to be "out of time"? That's an important consideration since time (as we know it) no longer exists in the same way when we are deeply absorbed in spiritual practice. If you take up the old textbook prescription for meditation and translate it into present-day activity, then you must pass through various stages of focus and concentration.

Fundamentally what you're doing first is learning to withdraw your attention from the outside world. In Sanskrit, this first step is referred to as *pratyahara*—the withdrawal of attention from sense-objects. The second step is called *dharana*, which generally means concentration. Now our focus of attention is principally internally based; as we become more practiced (as in what is called *ekagrata*, or one-pointed focus), we can keep our attention on a pinpoint or a flame for long periods (or, as in many ancient traditions, on a particular mantra or deity). Then we have entered what is traditionally referred to as *dhyana* or deep-rooted meditation. All these states intermingle as we gain connection through practice and more practice. The upshot of all this internalized energy and concentration then leads us to a state even beyond our normal take on meditation; for after much devoted practice, we are able to enter *samadhi*, which is a state of total absorption and integration. Here the mind is so deeply becalmed that whether there is the presence of thought or the absence of thought, utter calm reigns supreme, connected as we are with the indwelling spirit, that takes us way beyond ordinary awareness or contemplation.[18]

That's the outline of a traditional yogic meditation practice. For most of us, however, just learning to let go of ordinary states and breathe deeply, praying, or interacting with higher consciousness through journaling, reading (as in the practice of *Lectio Divina*—reading any prayer or scripture out loud at an extremely slow pace) is the basic "first course." Real practice, no matter what we choose to do, induces a state of calm and deep inner reflection. We can sing, pray, walk through a park or pathway, or simply sit in quiet meditation for any length of time desired.

Clearly there are multiple practices from which to choose. Lewis Richmond, a Buddhist writer and teacher, offers three practices from the Buddhist tradition that have been shown to generate greater happiness as we move through the aging process. He speaks about developing gratitude, generosity, and the reframing of life events.[19] As far as reframing is concerned, we place a lot of emphasis doing that kind of work as we engage the practice of "Telling a New Story" later in Chapter 13.

---

[18] BKS Iyengar (pp. 45-52)
[19] Richmond (*5 Spiritual Practices* online)

Choosing Spiritual Practices Aligned with Your Path

Among the practices mentioned by Richmond, gratitude may be the most elusive of all. In one moment, we're engaged, saying I'm grateful I can still get around, or I'm grateful my kids bought me one of those alert buttons, but in the next moment we've switched our focus back to the many ailments and complaints that are well within reach. Gratitude is something that needs to be taken on as a very conscious and deliberate practice; often I whisper things to myself, like how grateful I am for the massage I just received or for the fact that sparrows and chickadees like to gather and talk to each other on my porch.

The practice of generosity, of course, is central to most religious and spiritual traditions. Consider the three *T*s that are a given in many approaches to church membership, where you're frequently asked to pledge your *time, talent, and treasure* in support of the church. I like Richmond's slant on the issue, though, when he talks about a possible miracle drug to be dispensed:

> *One happiness study reported that if giving weren't free, drug companies could market a great new drug called "give back" instead of Prozac. It's scientifically proven: giving back and helping others makes us feel happier and more content. Giving is a universal spiritual value taught by every religion, and the desire to give back naturally increases as we age. It is part of our emerging role as community elders—something we can do into our sixties, seventies, eighties and beyond. Giving is truly a spiritual practice, and it naturally lifts our spirits.*[20]

Richmond adds curiosity and flexibility to the three key practices that he mentions on his list. Advising us not to get rigid or stuck in our ideas, he recommends adopting flexibility both as a physical activity but also as a means to move beyond obstacles:

---

[20] Richmond (*5 Spiritual Practices* online) (page 1)

> *With every reversal comes new opportunity. No matter what the issue, no matter how big the problem, there is always something constructive that you can do. Never give up, never let aging get the better of you.*[21]

Once again the question reverts to your desire and intention. What will inspire you to stay rooted in such practice? What do you hope to receive? Beyond stillness and peace, there is a very important effect, and it can be summed up as self-realization. Any practice that does not help us evolve our consciousness, raising awareness of who we are and what we offer others is not worthy of being called spiritual practice. Ultimately we are all moving (in our own way and within our own timing) toward complete freedom, or what the yogis call *moksha* or liberation. We seek freedom from any constraints, myths, or illusions that might contribute to our suffering and darkness. I love what Swami Kripalu used to tell us in his many talks at Kripalu Center when he visited back in the late seventies in Sumneytown, PA:

> *To read uplifting books or hear spiritual discourses is good. But to practice even a little is of utmost importance. The profound meaning of spiritual life is only grasped through personal practice.*[22]

Spiritual practice is not the only thing that helps us access this freedom; however, it offers distinct steps to harness our bodies and clear our minds so we can move onward. Therefore, if you were going to choose something that would light up your spirit and embolden movement along your spiritual path, what might you choose? Of all the practices that illuminate consciousness or raise energy, what do you imagine has your name written on it right now?

---

[21] Richmond, *Ibid*
[22] Levitt, ed., 2004 (page 138)

Chapter Seven

On Love, Relationship, and Keeping Your Heart Open

> *Without love, light cannot be kindled in our hearts, our homes, or in the world. Whatever scripture you may be reading is meaningless without love. The only guide on the true path—the only thing that draws another human being toward love—is love itself. Love is God's true ambassador in this world.*[23]

Every spiritual teacher in every religion, culture, or tradition invariably articulates thoughts and ruminations on the topic of love. Perhaps one of the most famous sayings in the Bible was summed up in John's Gospel (John 13:34), when he shared Jesus's new commandment:

> *I give you a new commandment that you love one another. Just as I have loved you, you also should love one another. By this everyone will know that you are my disciples if you have love for one another.*

As we travel our distinct spiritual pathways, it may be that finding the means to truly love others as well as ourselves will constitute the core of the greatest curriculum we will ever encounter in life. This simple four-letter word *love* probably has four million lessons

---

[23] Levitt, ed., 2004 (page 120)

or interpretations. We may discover the real meaning of love through its actual loss—or through the experience of betrayal or emptiness or denial of love. Out of what's missing or lost, gradually we find our way back to the center of love itself, which begins and ends within our own internal construction. The self-love that's drawn upon from within generates a force field that then transmits the same love outward to include others. In truth, it's not two separate things. Love is one thing only, and that is our ability to remain connected to Source. When we are deeply connected, it is easy, then, to emanate joy, gratitude, peace, kindness, and creative interaction with all beings.

My favorite little anecdote on love is excerpted from a 2023 online speech given by Sister Bhakti, member of the *Self-Realization Fellowship* in California. Speaking about how to begin creating spiritual relationships, she recounts a letter that a little girl once wrote to God. In it, the child said:

> *Dear God, It must be very hard for you to love ALL THE PEOPLE in the world. There's only four people in my family, and I just can't love them all the time...*[24]

Do we know anyone who has perfected the art of loving people all the time? That's the question. Like everything else we take on as we walk our spiritual path, love itself is not a static concern. It is not a *thing* but rather—a *practice* worthy of our time, effort, and dedication. And much like any other spiritual practice, we make different attempts, fall back, make more attempts, and then we forget, or have to renew our attention and effort. Love is rarely a done deal. It's more like, "try, try again."

---

[24] Sister Bhakti (Online Article)

On Love, Relationship, and Keeping Your Heart Open

Loving-kindness Meditation

The practice of loving-kindness meditation (or *Metta*, as it's known in Pali) originated centuries ago in Asia and has developed multiple forms as it has spread throughout the world. Its purpose is to build inner love and generosity of spirit in order to extend this unconditional love out to others. Loving-kindness meditation is not designed as an *exchange* but rather as an *offering*. It arises from a place of selflessness and as a practice gradually softens and releases barriers we may feel toward others or ourselves. That is why it is called *practice*; its roots go much deeper than the mere exchange of gifts or greetings.[25]

There are many different forms of loving-kindness practice. Anyone taking up this practice is free to rearrange words or sayings so that they resonate. The following are standard blessings:

- May I be safe. May you be safe. May all beings experience safety.
- May I be happy. May you be happy. May all beings experience happiness.
- May I be at peace. May you be at peace. May all beings experience peace.
- May I be healthy. May you be healthy. May all beings experience good health.
- May I live with ease. May you live with ease. May all beings experience ease.

As we repeat these blessings, in a sense we are building our unconditional "love muscles," which, given the nature of today's world, may have atrophied in some way. Originally, this practice was created with a layered effect:

---

[25] From the collected teachings of His Holiness the Dalai Lama

The Spiritual Path of Aging

- First, you offer blessings of peace, health, or happiness to yourself.
- Next, you extend the same blessings to a mentor or teacher.
- Next, you extend the same blessings to a friend, lover, or family member.
- Next, you offer these blessings to someone who's considered a *neutral* person.
- Next, you offer to one who is considered an enemy or difficult person.
- Finally, you offer these same blessings to all beings.[26]

The many benefits of this practice have to do with evoking peace, balance, and serenity within your mind and heart that naturally extend to others. Such benefits are connected to the ability to pivot—or shift your focus away from harmful or negative thoughts, returning to neutrality.

I love the brief anecdote in Joseph Goldstein's work, *Insight Meditation*, in which he talks about a difficult encounter for a meditation teacher, riding a rickshaw in India, who was accosted and practically dragged out of her rickshaw by a thief, but was finally saved by her friend. When she returned to her retreat center and shared about that violent encounter, her teacher exclaimed, "Oh, dear. With all the loving-kindness in your heart, you should have taken your umbrella and hit that man over the head."[27]

So there may be times when loving-kindness is just not applicable. After long practice, however, a broader shift occurs in which you naturally feel unconditional love for others. This does not mean you condone wrong actions, but simply that you are no longer willing to entrain with negative thought patterns, because you recognize their harmful effects. Instead, you live from a place of love and continue to generate heartfelt love to self and others. This practice

---

[26] From the collected teachings of His Holiness the Dalai Lama
[27] Goldstein, page 75

On Love, Relationship, and Keeping Your Heart Open

engenders true hope for the future and the sincere desire that "All beings may come to know love, peace, and safety," and additionally that "All beings may experience joy, harmony and blessing."[28]

> *Over a period of time, meditation develops a tremendous tenderness of heart. Although it is not always apparent in the day-to-day hindrances and ups and downs of practice, a softening of the mind and heart takes place that transforms the way we relate to others and ourselves. We begin to feel more deeply, and this depth of feeling becomes the wellspring of compassion.*[29]

---

[28] From the collected teachings of His Holiness the Dalai Lama
[29] Goldstein (page 147)

Chapter Eight

The New Paradigm of Love

I am indebted to Danielle Rama Hoffman, magnificent friend, spiritual teacher, and Supreme Channel of Light Beings, for her amazing work bringing us the latest news from Source. In the many years that I've known her, Danielle has a way of channeling Light Beings such as Thoth, Ancient Wisdom Teacher and Keeper of the Akashic records, as well as Isis, Yeshua, and many other Guides and Ascended Masters who help us grasp much more clearly the changes and transformations that we're facing. It is a true gift that Danielle shares magnanimously with all of us. I cannot tell you how much these teachings have opened my heart, expanded my consciousness, and changed the whole trajectory of my life experience.

For years, Danielle and the Guides have been teaching us how life has progressed from the Old Paradigm to a New Paradigm of consciousness. Although we may be familiar with these terms, the reality of this great shift may not have fully sunk in since we've lived under the influence of the "Old" for so long. However, the term *New Paradigm* fits perfectly here, since in the Old Paradigm our life experience was often divided between issues of *power over or power under*. In that environment everyone was not considered equal or worthy of the same benefits in life as others. However, the New Paradigm puts paid to that template, reminding us that we are all equal; we are all one in the spirit; and whether we're Beings of Light who are embodied or in spirit, we are all contributing simultaneously to the evolution in consciousness on this planet.

Learning about the changes precipitating this New Paradigm in consciousness helps catapult us into a new relationship with and understanding of love. It also helps us understand why the aging process and elders have been relegated to the sidelines (or indeed disappeared from view altogether…). What follows are a series of messages channeled by Danielle from Thoth and the Council of Light from 2018 through early 2023.[30]

> *You are blessed now with the opportunity to awaken dormant energies and frequencies of LOVE so you may use them more efficiently and effectively as a Being of Light incarnate. You are in the process of creating the most conducive environments for LOVE to be birthed—for LOVE to be actualized, and for LOVE to be more fully expressed in your life. This is not only LOVE of others (as is expected) but a great deepening into the LOVE present within your field of consciousness, directed to your own evolutionary progress.*

In the old paradigm, we were often caught up in what Thoth referred to as "separation consciousness":

> *Rooted in separation consciousness, the old paradigm scrambles the signal you're receiving from the Divine with slower vibrations like doubt and second-guessing. It's like trying to listen to your favorite big city radio station while driving through the country. The radio signal is coming through, but out in the boondocks, the reception gets spotty. The music starts to cut in and out. What you need instead is a way to receive a steady signal that never cuts out so you can count*

---

[30] Hoffman (DivineTransmissions.com)

on it no matter what. That way you get to keep humming along, no matter what environment you're in.

The key to receiving a steady signal from the Divine lies in expanding into your multidimensional nature so that you can receive it, not from your old paradigm vantage point (where the signal can be spotty and hard for you to trust) but from the Unity consciousness vantage point of your Divine Self. When you're able to do this, you receive guidance and you choose to act. There's no second-guessing or questioning required. You just know how to fully occupy your multidimensional space and operate in a vibrationally conducive environment regardless of what's happening around you.

In many ways, then, we must choose to move out of an old way of relating to life as we acknowledge and head into the New Paradigm, for it represents a total shift in consciousness. Like anything else, it requires steadfastness, practice, and occasionally the willingness to receive help from mentors, spiritual teachers, and in this case, support from one who lives and breathes this unified experience, such as our dear channel, Danielle Rama Hoffman:

As you pivot from being sourced from Separation consciousness to Source consciousness, to wholeness, and to knowing that all is well—old survival patterns may fight to survive and can get louder as they try to get your attention. However, it is time to allow those outdated ways of being to fall away and to be included back into the wholeness so that your consciousness is vibrating with your Source and with your Divine alchemy of unity.

*As you deepen your awareness that your consciousness is pivotal and can serve as a tool for shifting paradigms, you begin to have **aha** moments, which change the way you perceive your life in this incarnation. Be aware that actively utilizing your capacity to focus your consciousness, to be connecting and in* *communion with that which is uniquely you and yours, is a game changer. It's a quantum leap.*

These words land like poetry. At times they even feel like *scripture*. That is because their message is clearly sacred. It's important that we take them in stride and realize they serve to awaken our inner knowing about love's possibilities. Even when we find ourselves in "loveless" states, our capacity to pivot and return to a deeper connection is always present. The last thing we want to do is to turn things around and make ourselves wrong if we happen to wander into a moment of *separation*!

*Know that you already have what you need. You already know what to do. Yet the next step is to choose. Say to yourself: I **choose** to be the awakened consciousness that I am—the quantum consciousness that I am. As you turn on this consciousness we invite you to recognize, from a vibrational standpoint that you're humming; you're vibrating and in fact you're already living as the Source Being of Light that you are.*

This is a good time for awakening more and more of your capacity for love. Recognize that Awakened Love is the runway for the Being of Light that you are to become incarnate, to grow, shedding old ways of being, and finally moving into your most evolved and consecrated state of consciousness. For you are blessed now with the opportunity to awaken the dormant energies and frequencies of love.

You need to remember that you are Source and that you are in UNION with Source. Not only are you a magnificent giver of love, but it's important also to be a magnificent receiver of love. What you're moving into is a sacred act of love with and for yourself, as well as an unprecedented sacred act of love with and for others. This is confirmed as you acknowledge how much you are loved, cherished, and adored—witnessing the fullness of you being fully ignited.

The Spiritual Path of Aging

(Please note: All material in this chapter comes from a series of teachings channeled by Danielle Rama Hoffman, founder of DivineTransmissions.com. This author has attended multiple workshops both online and in person with Danielle and has come to treasure the messages relayed by such Light Beings as Thoth, Isis, Seshat, Yeshua, Anna, and many more. Quotes in this chapter as well as others in this text were all received in various transmissions by Danielle between 2018 and 2023.)

Chapter Nine

Transitions and Transformations

In a recent group experience I led for older people, one woman complained that despite her age, there was still so much she wanted to accomplish that her timeline to "get things done" felt shorter and shorter. She imagined being in a race against her living self while in fact death was waiting for her at the finish line.

What's still left undone is something we need to take into consideration. Before you depart this earthly life, what is yet to be accomplished? What regrets do you have about things left incomplete or undone? Of course, the opposite is also the case—we may in fact have run out of things to do or a sense of underlying purpose. That, too, needs to be considered. Many things will naturally fall by the wayside as we age; however, there are invariably things still in the "pipeline," awaiting our attention.

As a matter of fact, writing this book is a good example. After completing many different works earlier in life, I felt I was done with writing and the publishing process. Wrong! I had to revise my former view when I began hearing much of the unfinished business of elders—and could identify the same themes within myself.

So what's left for you to do? This may not be the time to apply to medical school, although I must counter my own argument by referring to one brave woman I knew who, at eighty three, decided she wanted to take up that lifelong dream and was accepted into Harvard Medical School! On the other hand, this may be a good time to clear the attic of all the trophies, mementos, and debris accumulated over the course of fifty or sixty years.

I appreciate the fact that toward the end of her long life, my mother decided to write a brief memoir, which she arranged to have published in a little booklet given only to surviving family members. It was her hope that we wouldn't lose sight of our history or the ancestors who prepared the way for all of us.

There are many ways to serve or be engaged in life. However, as we age we may need to become more focused and creative in our selections. For example, this may be a good time to volunteer to work with Lit Net, helping people learn how to read, or to work at the local school or hospital. Or this may be the time to take up a craft that has long puzzled or interested you. A woman I knew, who lost both her husband and her son in the same year, told me her one consolation in life was that she still had her lifelong weaving project and knitting to keep her busy. At the time she had taken up creating beautiful woven carpets and hanging tapestries to give to friends for Christmas and holidays.

As you think about it, what actions might help you feel fulfilled, and more easily engaged in the process of living? Sometimes it just amounts to a day-to-day decision, but the question that invariably precedes the final decision is this: Will I, or will I not *choose* to be engaged? Although he makes a rather intense statement, there is some truth in Kierkegaard's pronouncement:

> *It is very dangerous to go into eternity with possibilities which one has oneself prevented from becoming realities. A possibility is a hint from God. One must follow it.*[31]

It is helpful to put all of this into perspective, however. Though we may not be prepared to go *gently into that good night*, we are still moving through a series of life transitions, each of which is marked

---

[31] Kierkegaard (Online quote)

by a tiny invisible tag that lights up in our minds, *Is this the one? Is this new diagnosis going to be the one that leads to death and dying? Is it this bump or lump in my body? Or is it this terrible break-up, this divorce, this change in vision or hearing, or this loss of a capacity we'd taken for granted?*

When working with groups or individual clients, I often defer to William Bridges' seminal work, providing an excellent breakdown of the main elements present in any great transition: *Making Sense of Life's Transitions*. It's helpful to sort out where we are among the many life changes and to settle into the differing qualities and conditions represented by each of Bridges' three main stages.[32]

Although the three stages may overlap at times, they each have a different purpose, a different energetic quality, and a way of preparing for the next stage to unfold. Put succinctly, the three stages include:

- **Endings**—saying goodbye to a way of life, an epoch, an experience, or even a personal identity.
- **Neutral Zone**—a time of germination, which is largely inchoate and undefined. We must pass through this "zone" in order to integrate the prior process. There is no defined "what to do or how to be" in this stage. It is an interval, a time to push the pause button, and to allow our lives to be renewed through ritual, repetition, and spiritual practice.
- **New Beginnings**—when we've become clear that the old is no longer acceptable, then we know we are free to move on. Starting over again in a whole new way, we take up new challenges and feel invigorated by this fresh start and new way to engage in our life experience.

Endings and beginnings, with emptiness and germination in between. That is the shape of the transition periods in our lives,

---

[32] Bridges (*Making Sense of Life's Transitions*)

and these times come more frequently in adulthood and cut more deeply than most of us imagined they would. But the same process is also going on continuously in our lives. As humankind once knew and celebrated, the same rhythm puts us to sleep at night and wakes us in the morning...It takes us through the turning year, around to an ending which opens out to a new beginning. And so it is with our lives—a dozen little endings, hardly noticed in the day-to-day rush, plunge us into little wildernesses; a dozen little beginnings, taking shape in confusion and emerging unexpectedly into clear form.[33]

---

[33] Ibid (page 150)

Chapter Ten

Managing "Old Age Loneliness..."

I'm sitting here on a beautiful spring afternoon all by myself. This is not an unusual situation for me. Generally, when I'm not working my various jobs, attending church, or going to concerts or other events, I'm by myself. Now, don't get me wrong, I do have wonderful friends a few miles away, or fifty miles away, or in Florida. And of course my extended family lives in Philadelphia. But I have come to that peculiar crossroads many will relate to, which I have dubbed "Old Age Loneliness." It's not for a lack of reaching out or making plans. It's not that my bad mood sends people away. It's just that I'm older than most of my friends, and none of them have the same need for connection or companionship as I do. In addition, two of my dearest friends have died. Others live too far away to join together for a friendly dinner on a Friday night.

This is a reality many of us who live alone must face within the aging process. Once I was married; I'm not anymore. I never wound up having kids. A few relationships later, I discovered that I actually preferred living alone. However, that was more than twenty years ago, when I was still deeply engaged in multiple communities, working at Kripalu Center, beginning also at Canyon Ranch, and deeply involved with the ballroom dance community in western Massachusetts. But let's face it; if you're not in assisted living or in a nursing home and you live all by yourself, it's a bit of a rough go nowadays for old folks. And even within those communities, loneliness is rampant.

The Spiritual Path of Aging

I had an interesting chat with a dear friend (who's twelve years younger than I am). Forcing myself to be perfectly honest, I leveled with her about how hard it was to connect with her or wait until she called or made some attempt for us to get together. In our conversation, I outlined what I imagined were her real priorities in terms of connection: first of all, her husband was top of the list (which made perfect sense, especially since they're the only ones left in their home). Second in order was the care of her dog and two cats—an ancient Tom and a very young frisky kitten. Third was establishing connection with her two adult children, one of whom was living in Providence, RI, and the other in Philadelphia. Fourth were her aging parents, whom she visited every few months out in California. And fifth were her closest friends over the years. Sixth were friends she's gotten to know in the past few years which evidently includes me… She nodded that this was close to the truth for her, and I got it. Being fifth or sixth string varsity meant that I was rarely called upon to be *in the game*.

And it's nobody's fault. It's certainly not hers; after all, she does have all these commitments and any day of the week she can be located in Rhode Island or as far away as California. But neither is it my fault that I'm older and don't have that many choices—no spouse, no children, grandkids—and in effect, very few friends my age who want to add my name to their dance card.

Of course there are many variables in this situation, and even those surrounded by family or close friends often find themselves alone or at odds with each other. That's because it's very hard to adapt to the physical and psychological changes that come as a result of the aging process and at the same time gently adapt to being alone—whether all by yourself or in the midst of your "crowd." (It's amusing to me when I think of the various ways we define our groups: a herd of cows, a flock of birds, a colony of ants—and my favorite—*a murder of crows*. I have a feeling that for us elders, that last category pertains more than any other.)

So the truth is, whether living alone or ensconced within family, or in any setting, we must come to grips with the fundamental experience of loneliness. Of course it isn't as if this is the first go-round. Certainly we've been lonely as teenagers, or young adults or anywhere along the way to old age. It's just that if you add old age into the equation, then it's doubly hard to adapt. That's why I've called it Old Age Loneliness. It's not that easy to dismiss. Nor can it be resolved, given that we've outgrown most of our community, or they've left us, or, frankly, we're just not that easy to get along with. On this count, my sister and I both agree. That is because even though we may be desperate for companionship, at the same time we may actually repel some people, given that often they can't resonate with where or who we are, and we're no longer at the stage where we want to placate or manage their discomfort. How's that for a nice *triple whammy*?

There can be something harsh and relentless about this issue of loneliness; it just doesn't find an easy resolution, no matter how you approach it. What is being asked for is to find a way to be present—and more than that—if at all possible—to *befriend* that lonesome state. I certainly haven't achieved that yet, although I love the ideas presented by Pema Chödrön in a beautiful article recently published online from *Lion's Roar*:

> *We are fundamentally alone, and there is nothing anywhere to hold on to. Moreover, this is not a problem. In fact, it allows us to finally discover a completely unfabricated state of being. Our habitual assumptions—all our ideas about how things are—keep us from seeing anything in a fresh, open way. We say, "Oh yes, I know." But we don't know. We don't ultimately know anything. There's no certainty about anything. This basic truth hurts, and we want to run away from it. But coming back and relaxing with something as familiar as loneliness is good discipline for realizing the profundity of the unresolved*

moments of our lives. We are cheating ourselves when we run away from the ambiguity of loneliness.[34]

In addition, Thoth (whom you met in Chapter 8) encourages us that along with shifting our perspective comes an inevitable shift in our vibrational reality:

*You stand as you and only you. You move from being separate from yourself to being **with** yourself. You move from being disconnected to being connected. There's a shift from seeking, longing, and searching, to being in the same vibrational proximity. It's a feeling of being met in a unique way: only it's you who meets yourself, and you then enter a vibration of true partnership and true equality with yourself.*[35]

Both of these are very lofty goals that will take us to a brand new and highly transcendent experience—not only having to do with loneliness, but also with issues that may stand in the way of our freedom, wholeness, and full engagement in this process called living.

---

[34] Chödrön (page 3)
[35] Hoffman: DivineTransmissions.com

Chapter Eleven

The Fierce Art of Letting Go

This brings us to the heart of the matter—or at least the next step in attaining that quality of freedom. A synonym for the aging process (that most of us elders recognize as highly important) is the term *letting go*. There is nothing quite like this time in life; no matter what you've achieved—how you feel—how you look—or how you're occupied, the fundamental action you're called to take part in is what I call the "Fierce Art of Letting Go."

I'd like to acknowledge the Ancient Egyptian Goddess Sekhmet who combines a loving heart with a fierce physical presence: she shares a woman's body with a lion's head! And she has the capacity to transition fully between her human self and her lioness self—in order to carry out her unusual and very "fierce" task of helping you release old habits, fears, or traumas. I am deeply grateful to Nicki Scully and her incredible shamanic work helping us journey through the fierce letting go that happens when you meet up with Sekhmet.[36] Her process is much deeper, more exotic, and in some ways preposterous, for she is going to *ingest* you physically from head to toe, and then do the clearing work while you stay energetically captive inside her belly. It's a rather unorthodox way to clear things, you might say—unlike any kind of therapy one might encounter in the western world!

---

[36] Scully (In her work *Sekhmet*...)

And yet this ancient series of rituals associated with the Goddess Sekhmet outlines a process that even for us today needs to be strenuous, assiduously attended to, and in many ways inclusive of the preposterous or the absurd. We need to cleanse our energy fields of the baggage we've been carrying around for lifetimes. But who knew that in the ancient Egyptian methodology our old, tired out or disgusting parts might be consumed and digested in the belly of a lion?

This is a core shamanic practice; it's also a symbol for what we must be willing to go through in order to reclaim our essence—that which is forever linked with our Divine Nature—our Inner Being, our precious Soul. However, in this day and age, we are not necessarily called upon to travel the Nile or meet with Sekhmet in her temple in order to do the work of "fierce letting go." We can take a similar pilgrimage on our own, perhaps with a partner, a friend, a therapist, or by invoking the presence of a Light Being or Spiritual Guide. First, follow Thoth's suggestions:

> *Take a few breaths to clear your mind. Now feel that the light, the joy, the depth of who you are is being both illuminated and set free at the same time. You are in the hands of Spirit. Your energy field is widening, deepening, allowing, expressing, and including everything back into the wholeness. Feel yourself fully immersed now in the frequencies of love, light, and evolved consciousness.*

So now it's my time for centering. It's my time for letting go. As I sit in my meditation room, however, I am interrupted by lingering thoughts coupled with angst and sadness that descended after completing the prior chapter on loneliness. Some realizations are hard to shake. Some are persistent and revisit often, as in this issue of loneliness. And when I feel burdened by leftover feelings or repetitive nagging thoughts, inevitably they are my signal that there's more work to do. In that instant I recognize that I'm already *in process*. So I go back to the beginning. I go back to establishing Witness Consciousness as I sit in meditation.

Breathe, relax, feel, watch, and allow. This small set of directions has very deep implications for letting go. The first step is simple: breathe. Just breathe. It's not so easy when I'm caught up in the incipient feeling of emotions rising up; nevertheless, I allow the breath to lengthen and deepen as I sit.

The second step rides piggyback on the slower breathing process I've initiated. It's time for me to relax. Relaxation isn't called in so I can go to sleep or ignore the deeper issue. I use relaxation as an aid to submerging deeper while at the same time calling in more global awareness. Besides, knowing that any issue I'm working with is going to bring up a variety of strong emotions, I want to be relaxed and aware—in such a way that enables me to be present with my experience rather than resist or push back. So as I soften in my body and allow my heart and mind to be in receiving mode, naturally feelings of grief and sadness arise and become more persistent.

Now the real work of feeling begins. In this case I begin to perceive Loneliness as a real entity—a living being who has a separate existence independent of my own and yet impinges deeply on my reality. So I wish to investigate her. (I often relate to Loneliness as feminine.) Mostly I choose to push her away. After all, she can be dark, moody, and sometimes life-threatening. But today my mood is softening, and I want to get to the root of my fear and sadness. So I officially call upon the presence of Loneliness to help me sort out this conundrum.

Loneliness Shows Up:

Lo: Well, well—I'm here! So you want to get to know me?

Jo: Yes, please, I need your help!

Lo: That's fine, though you do call on me a lot lately.

Jo: Well, you show up, don't you?

The Spiritual Path of Aging

Lo: Yes, but I have to advise you that you take much too seriously this business of always needing someone to validate your existence!

Jo: But you can't deny my experience! Can't you see it?

Lo: I'm not blind, darling. But yes, fill me in if you need to.

Jo: I feel adrift. I feel left by the wayside when a friend never answers her phone or takes her good old time responding to my recent email. What am I? Chopped liver? Then another friend answers me a week after I've sent her three different options for a get-together: a movie, a dinner, or a concert coming up on a Saturday afternoon. Then I finally receive an email with no apology, simply acknowledging the "the week got away from her." Meanwhile here I am sitting alone and troubled. Why can't people communicate in a timely fashion?

Lo: That's a sign of the times. It's pretty standard—unless you prefer to scroll through a dozen texts.

Jo: No, I hate that. Of course, I understand that this weighs more heavily on me now than ever because I have fewer contacts and fewer invitations than ever. It's also the case that many of my friends (who may have families or simply be more connected in other ways) don't have the same itch or need to be connected.

Lo: Well, that's all well and good. You describe things well! However, you neglect to understand how your fear and confusion about real contact are sitting right now on the edge of your energy field—getting in the way. I don't say this as a judgment about you. After all, I am Loneliness. I know what it's all about. But I attend when the energy strikes or the fear rises to the surface…

Jo: Yes, I get it. I can almost see you in your black dress and wide brimmed hat.

Lo: It's true, my dear—I am very fashionable; make no mistake about it. I came at your call, didn't I?

Jo: Yes, and you're a royal pain in the ass; trust me.

Lo: I may be a pain—but you're the one sitting on your ass. Your constant lament that there's no place to go, no one to accompany you, and no one calling to see how you are keeps ringing in my ears—

Jo: I hate it when you keep throwing that back in my face!

Lo: Oh, but I do it with a proud purpose!

Jo: Which is?

Lo: Lack, lack, lack—do you hear the clickety-clack of those train wheels rolling down the track? It's all about your focus of attention my dear, clickety-clack, lickety-lack—lack, lack, lack.

Jo: That's just great. I'm sitting here all alone and you're taunting me. You're insinuating that my focus needs to shift to something else? I must go to some other time or place but not this moment?

Lo: Exactly! You've had times yesterday, earlier today, and even tomorrow when you're with others or engaged in some writing project where there's absolutely no need to focus so wholeheartedly on *clickety-clack; now I'm in lack.*

Jo: So my focus is off, is that it?

Lo: Absolutely! You can turn in a different direction.

Jo: Oh God! You make it seem like child's play! But it's actually a heart-rending experience.

Lo: Maybe because you keep repeating it! But after all is said and done, feeling Lonely is just a thought form!

Jo: What?

The Spiritual Path of Aging

Lo: You heard me. I am the result of your thinking and cogitating. You create me just like you create everything else.

Jo: Oh God, I can't believe this.

Lo: That's the whole problem, my dear!

Jo: Great! I just need to shift my habit of thinking! What you're insinuating is that I must totally negate or deny my reality!

Lo: Reality, Pee-ality, Schmee-ality; don't be so identified with this fake moment in time!

Jo: Why do you call it fake?

Lo: Because you have chosen to forget your true identity and have instead settled for this fake version of you—this upset, crying, grieving—big *pouting baby* that you are!

Jo: Wow. You really know how to put a person at ease.

Lo: I'm not trying to put you at ease or into any other state of being. Remember: it was you who called me here in the first place. And frankly I could be in so many other places that are juicier than here right now.

Jo: What do you mean by that?

Lo: Well, you see, some folks actually worship the ground I stand on. They don't question my presence at all; they want nothing more than to have me show up, so they can take to the bottle or the telly or just sit and cry. Can you imagine?

Jo: Phew. I'm overjoyed. You're not satisfied with just putting me down; you have to drag along everyone else who's ever been lonely!

Lo: But don't you see? That's my calling! And if I want to keep my job, then there must be reasons for me to be present. Now let's get back to your dilemma. Why do I show up so frequently for you? Better yet, why do you call on me?

Jo: Because I feel unappreciated, unrecognized, and unseen. It's very strange, but every time a call or invitation—or any kind of connection gets dropped or is evaded by someone I hold dear, I feel like I've been thrown under the bus, or left by the side of the road.

Lo: But it's just a call or an email!

Jo: That's true. But no response in my world means death to me. It means the relationship is dead. Or I'm dead. Or soon enough I will have the experience of being thrown out the window or trampled to death. Over and over I could just scream, "Don't leave me here! Don't abandon me! Please don't let me die!"

Lo: And that's your core experience—the one that's waiting to be explored and expelled, my dear. So relax. Breathe. Let it go. Yes, it's okay to cry now. You need to grasp that you are neither abandoned nor left here to die. You are very much loved and very deeply connected—not only here on Earth but in multiple dimensions of Spirit extending out into the Universe and to the galaxies beyond. It's time for you to release this old illusion. Yes, good. Let it go…

Jo: (Finding it hard to breathe, with tears running down my cheeks.) What's happening? Is it shifting?

Lo: Yes, indeed. You've moved it a bit. But continue to work on remembering your true connection! Now please excuse me, but I hear someone calling; it's time for me to go.

Jo: (Still crying.) Goodbye and—and thank you!

Phew, what a visit! Leave it to Loneliness to tell it like it is. Yet in the stark reality of meeting with her face-to-face, so to speak, I have to say that I do feel somewhat unburdened by all of this. Who knew?

It's fascinating to see how our hidden fears or traumas often hearken back to the initial and all-pervading fear that this loneliness (or whatever else *this* is) is going to be the death of us. We're under attack! That's why some type of "Fierce Letting Go" is the most practical agenda for moving forward, along with what Chödrön referred to as accepting the "ambiguity" of loneliness and being able relax into it. That reminds me of these words of Alberto Villoldo, shaman and writer extraordinaire, who frequently joined us at Kripalu Center guiding us through magical shamanic journeys:

> *In order to really live, you must overcome the death that was meant for you. That means all the fears and limiting beliefs that suppress the life force. Life is not predatory in the shamanic tradition. When you step beyond death, you learn the journey of wholeness—or the way back home. So retrieve the elements of your soul that represent your becoming. When you make a connection with your power, then your becoming begins to track you. You're not only the hunter; you're hunted. The mystery of your being now begins to track you.*[37]

Whether you feel like a hunter right now or like the one who's one being hunted, consider the following questions. They may become part of the framework for your own shamanic work and for the journey that takes you back to your essence:

- In the process of growing older, what do you feel you've been forced **to give up**, recognizing that you don't really want to stop doing or experiencing it?
- In the process of growing older, what have you in fact **let go of,** (even though with some regret) recognizing that it's not in your best interest to hold onto or continue this activity?
- What still remains with you as a challenge and might perceivably be something requiring some Fierce Letting Go on your part?

---

[37] Villoldo (online Quote)

- In the process of growing older, what have you taken on—that is a source of joy or may be some old dream you had never been able to realize in earlier years that's now become your reality?
- In this moment of many transitions how would you characterize your present state? Are you principally saying goodbye as in witnessing certain Endings, or are you welcoming in some New Beginning? Or perhaps you may feel it's more of a mixed design, neither ending nor beginning anything but lingering more in something akin to the Neutral Zone?
- Besides a growing awareness of your mortality, what is the **hardest thing** for you to accept about the aging process?
- What **positive shifts** have you noticed? What are you now letting **in** or doing in a way that truly supports your spiritual progress?

Chapter Twelve

Examining Beliefs about Aging

There's so much to look forward to as we age—don't you think? We find multiple adjustments in how we approach life, coupled with the grief, loss, and awareness of our newfound limitations. Up to this point, we've been exploring a good bit of the downside of aging. That's because it is very much consistent with what we witness and are surrounded by—both in our personal experience and that of friends, relatives, and the extended society we live in. However, it's important to see things in a broader context.

Having watched a podcast of a 102-year-old physician named Dr. Gladys McGary, I was struck by the upbeat quality of her presentation; after all, she speaks with the expertise of at least twenty-three years more living than I've gotten around to. In addition, she adds many positive notes about her aging patient concerns. Considered the mother of holistic medicine, Gladys takes a very balanced approach with her aging population and outlines six secrets or ways to enjoy life and move more gracefully through the aging process. Succinctly put, her secrets include understanding the following:

> *(1) Living itself is an amazing thing; (2) Life is a blessing; (3) We're here for a reason; (4) Life has to move, so you can grow;*

Examining Beliefs about Aging

(5) We don't get over things, because life is hard; and (6) Love is the greatest healer.[38]

Although these may sound simplified, or perhaps a bit too easy, still it's important to reconsider in the light of the good doctor's aging process. How many of us will actually make it to 102? For the rest of us, there is an important turning point when we come to realize that we've been around a long time and want to extract the meaning from our lived experience—or possibly *make* new meaning from all that we've lived. As we embrace more of a spiritual perspective, then, our bold task is to look beneath the surface to understand the concepts and beliefs that shape our fundamental approach to and expectation of the aging process. If we skip back to Chapter Eight, we are reminded of the distinction between the Old and New Paradigms of consciousness. This can be helpful in noticing if we're still working within the old "operating system," instead of upgrading to the new one.

There are many examples of contrast or differences in how we perceive one another, but they're essentially rooted in unconscious patterning. In essence, the Old Paradigm was based in duality—the sense that we're separate from everything and everyone, and there's no uniting principle except for hardship and struggle, especially vis-à-vis the aging process. However, the New Paradigm refutes that positioning. It's not that old age suddenly becomes a joyous entertainment and something to look forward to (rather than a *shit show*), it's just that we discover a key element in all our limitations has to do with the limitations in our belief systems.

Now here's where it gets tricky. Understanding that our beliefs are the building blocks of our reality can become the source of either pain or pleasure. We may feel pain, guilt, or grief about our condition if we resort to blaming ourselves for what's created. On the other hand, pleasure and true freedom can arise from the notion

---

[38] Dr. McGary (online podcast)

that we're at the helm. We have greater potency and creative power around our aging process than we ever imagined—whether physical, mental, emotional, or spiritual in nature. It is not a judgment; it's an invitation.

The invitation is there, not only in relation to how we age, but also in relation to how we consider our input into all aspects of our lives. It's easy to blame our culture, our parents, our crazy world, or anything other than ourselves for the sorry state of our bodies and minds. And yet, if there's just a brief glimpse into the creative possibilities inherent in our consciousness, the portal can be crossed that will shift our overall experience.

The New Paradigm proclaims that we're all equal. We're all connected through Source. As a matter of fact, we are all Source. Which means that latent or unexplored uses of our minds, imagination, and mystical knowledge can open us to new directions. But we have to get over the idea that "life happens" and we're just the "victim of circumstances." That is the fundamental act of pivoting that the New Paradigm asks of us.

> *Your body is the basic product of your creativity on a physical level. From its integrity all other constructions in your lifetime must come…You create yourselves on a daily basis, changing your form according to the incalculable richness of your multitudinous abilities… Your beliefs about age, therefore, will affect your body and all of its capacities.*[39]

Since I am an *oldster*, I am grateful that I landed on Earth during the years referred to as the New Age—the time for flower children and longhaired hippies to do their walkabout. I am especially grateful for a long-ago introduction to channeling, especially in the lengthy messages Jane Roberts brought forth from the entity called Seth. Although I am certainly an heir to all the gifts and perils of

---

[39] Roberts (page 160)

Examining Beliefs about Aging

American culture, I am happy that way back in the sixties and seventies, I got a taste of an alternate view—and that is our ability to create our own experience, independent of what others think or do, and independent also of our prior conditioning. But to recognize that takes an act of courage—and the willingness to wake up! It doesn't mean that we "hold ourselves responsible" for any failures or mishaps. It doesn't mean we can now shift the blame from society or our family or our culture to ourselves. It means we have the chance to determine that what we're living and experiencing mirrors the *beliefs* we hold about our reality. And that leads us to the possibility of telling a brand-new story about our life experience.

Chapter Thirteen

Tell a New Story

> *Whenever you feel dissatisfied, question the 'story' you're telling yourself about the nature of that experience. You are capable of changing virtually anything in your life.*[40]

Despite all we know about our creative powers, it's still mind-boggling how often we find ourselves living in the space of delusion. Over and over we succumb to a kind of self-hypnosis based on the narrative we repeat to ourselves describing our daily life experience. It's very subtle; it's very deep. And by that I mean, so deeply embedded in our psyche and consciousness that we're hardly aware we're following the same story, agreeing word-for-word with what we've told ourselves was true eons ago. Unconsciously we've been narrating what to expect, what to fear, what to hope for, and what will never happen, based on old scripts, old conditioning, and a lack of clarity about who's really the *author* of our experience.

Even though I know this, and I teach this, and I have this awareness lodged somewhere between the right and left hemispheres of my brain—still, I frequently catch myself in the middle of worshiping a series of lies about who I am or what I'm capable of. Two sentences recently showed up online that made me smile. "Everyone lies continually. That's because no one has access to or

---

[40] Roberts (Fans of Seth webpage)

is capable of accurately recalling life's events."[41] Perhaps the worst lies we tell ourselves are about our handicaps, our misfortune, our failures or our lack of creativity.

My main task in life seems to be reminding myself over and over again that I am capable of creating miracles—that my life itself is a miracle. Most people can remember the way John's Gospel mimics the same words God speaks in Genesis—how "In the beginning was the word and the word was with God, and the word **was** God." It's too bad we haven't accepted the real potential inherent in those words, for in fact they point to the universality of our Creation, the Sovereignty of our Actions, and the fact that what we speak (and think about and continue to narrate to ourselves) is the signal for what we're bringing about, now and in the future.

It is time to tell a new story. That might mean to dream a new dream. It might mean begin a new inquiry, or question if what we're living is a match to who we are or what our divine purpose on Earth is. Although our purpose generally remains unchanged through time, the forms and expressions it takes may shift or change based on what we've learned and what we now need to bring forth. I particularly love this quote from Eugene Kennedy—psychologist, writer, and former professor at Loyola University in Chicago:

> *Renewing ourselves does not demand that we remake ourselves entirely, but rather that, like the earth itself, we draw on the life that is already present—the possibilities that survive, and we give them a chance to grow and flourish.*[42]

Of course, the story that we repeat to ourselves is highly conditioned by what we've been told or led to believe, particularly about the difficulties of the aging process. "You'll lose it all." "You just can't do what you did when you were twenty." "The worst part is when you can't do things for yourself and have to have someone

---

[41] Roberts (Fans of Seth webpage)
[42] Kennedy (From AZquotes online)

help you." "Old age ain't for sissies." "It's best not to live so long that senility's approaching…"

What's interesting to me are comments on aging made more than fifty years ago to a small group of people listening to Jane Roberts channeling Seth in Elmira, New York. Many are familiar with some of these earliest channeled teachings that add a whole new perspective on human life and human beliefs. Basically, what Seth pointed out was that our awareness and knowledge of aging was clouded by our societal perceptions, fears, and conditioning. But the most important thing he conveyed was that an expansion in consciousness occurs as we grow older, echoing similar events that have occurred during adolescent years. Most people would naturally suppress such expansiveness, since a shift in focus or flights of fancy might be equated with senility rather than with creativity or new understandings. This blew my mind—speaking of expanding one's consciousness…

> *When it is time, then, the individual begins to see beyond temporal life, to open up dimensions of awareness that in your terms he or she could not afford while involved in the intense physical focus of normal adult life. Unfortunately the personality has no system of beliefs, as a rule, to support such an expansion…*[43]

It amazes me that with all the rigor and scientific research on brain function and the awareness that our brain cells may not be dying but potentially even proliferating as we age, no one has latched onto Seth's significant statements about expansion. And who even considers our later years as a time for inventiveness, creativity, or enhanced spiritual focus?

> *However, this is one of the most creative, valuable aspects of your lives. Instead, the old are made to feel useless in your*

---

[43] Roberts (page 254)

Tell a New Story

> *society... There are no teachers to guide you. Old age is a highly creative part of living... even the chemical and hormonal changes that occur are conducive to spiritual and psychic growth at that time. But joyful affirmation is denied to the old because of your system of beliefs.* [44]

From all of this it's clear that we must begin refining or altering our perception of aging and what's possible for our sixty, seventy, eighty, ninety, or one hundred plus years of living. I totally love the summary of elder achievements, pulled together in the *Journal of Aging and Health* demonstrating that aging creative people lived longer and dealt better with stress.[45] Among many of the notables outlined was Agatha Christie who at age eighty-four oversaw the revision of *Murder on the Orient Express* and wrote until she was eighty-six. Henri Matisse, impressionist painter, created his famous cutouts in his eighties. Verdi composed his comic opera *Falstaff* at age eighty, and Martha Graham, founder of her well-known modern dance group, continued dancing until she was seventy-five and choreographed her last work at age ninety-six. It's wonderful to hear about these and other creative elders, for they clearly disprove the notion of inevitable decline associated with aging. At the same time they give us a window into creative pursuits and a tiny inkling of possibilities we might consider relevant to our own aging process. Who knew?

We must come back to listening deeply—not so much to others as to ourselves and to the quality of narrative we've unconsciously been spinning about our lives. If the actual story is unclear, it's easy to discover its main theme by observing the outcome. Consider what shows up day-to-day in your life and also what fails to show up, even if it's what's really wanted.

---

[44] Roberts (page 254)
[45] Article: Do Creative People Live Longer?

Of course there are times in life when our awareness is not quite up to speed—either about our story or the results we're actually experiencing. This is not really a problem. That's because there are other ways we can learn and, in a sense, "turn up the volume." This happened not so long ago when I was feverishly at work finishing the end chapters of this book while also working overtime at two different jobs. I had so many things on my plate that my "plate" talked back to me. Hence, I call this episode:

Message from a Sausage

That particular morning, I had been up since 4 a.m. scribbling out the main details to be included in the book's acknowledgments. Suddenly, I looked at the clock and realized I was going to be late for work (for the first of my two jobs that day…). With no time for a regular breakfast, I just threw one of those big fat sausages (made with garlic and spinach) into the oven and rushed to get dressed and send out a few more emails. When I finally sat down to eat, I cut into the sausage and some piping hot fat from its interior immediately shot into my face and dribbled down my cheek. OUCH! I had to stop everything to find some burn ointment, and when I looked in the mirror and saw the big red blotch, all I could think of was how stupid I had been. But as I hurried out to my car, I realized that the sausage (like everything else in the universe) was trying to tell me something. Simply stated, the message was, "Slow down, baby, you're burnt out. You better find a way to turn down the heat…"

Of course, not all of us receive our lessons from a sausage—or even from breakfast as a whole. But life does have a way of tapping us on our shoulders (or burning our faces) so that we become aware of how we've been living. Once our awareness is keen, then, as described earlier in terms of witness consciousness, we can show up as the *witness*—the one who first feels the "burn," then observes its origin with compassion, releasing all sense of attachment or resentment to emerge into a place of neutrality. That creates a portal into freedom from past restrictions and limitations.

However, following that thread may mean giving up trying to "fix" or "clear" the past. This brings us full circle. We return to Thoth's message about shifting from the Old to the New Paradigm of Consciousness:

> *The Old Paradigm notion of trying to focus on clearing things doesn't work because nothing ever gets unstuck; it just recycles back over and over again. It exists eternally in a SLOWER vibration, and as you move into a HIGHER vibration, though the slower vibration still exists, your vantage point is in a higher realm. You have the capacity to bend negativity to be in the same location as Unity Consciousness! Where you're coming from changes, and with it the experience of so much more joy, equanimity, and happiness. If you're in a state of Wholeness, then that which you feel separate from will get included into that which is moving at a higher vibration, and it becomes part of your life.*

A lot has to do with energy and vibration, as Thoth informs us. Whatever story we may be devoted to is invariably a reflection of our dominant energy pattern. So you can see from my "sausage face" that I was pretty well scrambled (but without the eggs), and that that event clearly displayed the narrative of my life for the moment. Fortunately, some narratives only last a "moment" in Earth time. Others go on for years. The story we wish to recreate will be of greater benefit if it's in alignment with a higher state of consciousness—and thus a higher vibration. When we have reflected on our narrative, turned the corner into heightened awareness, and achieved a greater degree of calm and inner reflection, the resulting freedom points us in the direction of exciting new choices. Dispensing with the old hypnotic story, we take on a fresh new narrative, which hopefully is more life giving, more energizing and much more empowered than anything we've told ourselves in the past. When that happens, it's like a breath of fresh air wafts through. We remember that we are in fact Creators and can ignite the divine qualities of Creation any time that we choose. As Jane Roberts again reminds us, channeling Seth:

> *More than anything else, your soul is an unending source of Creation. It is the most highly motivated, most highly energized, and most potent unit of consciousness in this universe. Even in this moment, your soul is at work creating new worlds.* [46]

---

[46] Roberts (page 255)

Chapter Fourteen

Enlightened Elders

What does it mean to be enlightened? And how can it possibly be associated with or attributed to the aging process? As we spoke about earlier, being enlightened has to do with bringing more light into a situation. Light is a vibration—a pulsation of energy. Thus, the more you light up your awareness, the higher your vibrational frequency. And in some ways, the higher your vibration, the more you yourself lighten up!

Many scholars and scriptures, elaborate on this theme, and some, such as the *Diamond Sutra* from the Buddhist tradition, offer a very simple, paired down vision of enlightenment:

> *When I attained Absolute Perfect Enlightenment, I attained absolutely nothing. That is why it is called Absolute Perfect Enlightenment. After enlightenment you are still the same as you were before. There is no mind and there is no truth. You are simply free from unreality and delusion.*[47]

Many texts also allude to the act that loving others unconditionally is associated with being enlightened. Acts of loving-kindness can then be seen as part of a very high frequency or vibration—in essence a heightened state of consciousness. In other words, being loving is a way of bringing in more light and thus helping us become enlightened. Of course, in some traditions there is no such

---

[47] Mitchell (page 35)

The Spiritual Path of Aging

thing as "becoming." The assumption is that we already are enlightened. Whether we're tuned into it or not, practicing loving-kindness, as outlined in Chapter Seven, kindles greater awareness, along with greater compassion and understanding—which is very much the core message that His Holiness the Dalai Lama brings to the world:

> *Genuine compassion is cultivated when we recognize two aspects of existence: the first is a deep insight into how suffering is the nature of life in the greater cycle of existence, and the second is to realize the sameness of ourselves and others. We all have the natural tendency to seek happiness and avoid suffering. These two factors give rise to a true sense of responsibility to work for the benefit of others, which leads us to the experience of genuine compassion on behalf of all beings.*[48]

To further understand the nature of enlightenment, we need to return to what the Guides have offered us, distinguishing the Old Paradigm from the New Paradigm in consciousness. Above all, it is an evolving process. It is also a cyclical event. Just as we hope to recycle those things that are no longer useful on a material level, the same kind of recycling occurs at the level of spirit. It is a lengthy process for humankind, and it is one that we've been engaged in not just for a few centuries—but thousands of years.

The following are thoughts and suggestions that emerged in a recent sitting that I had with the Council of Light and my Guides:

> *In the Old Paradigm, as you recall, there was always an imbalance of power and a struggle to be better than, stronger than, or certainly not worse than. So consider how this might relate to the elders in your society. Due to diminished capabilities, illness, or mental decline, old people were soon*

---

[48] His Holiness the Dalai Lama (page 61)

relegated to the power under designation. It was not a conscious or thought-out process. Rather, it was part of the overall momentum throughout centuries, shifting awareness in different directions. If you were old, or a woman, or poor, or spoke a different language, or had different-colored skin, then you were easily sorted out and placed into those lower categories.

But this was not always the case. In earlier societies, indeed even among some Indigenous groups extant today, there are those who revere their elders and take good care of them. Old people were considered to be sages, mentors, and in fact, the repository of all knowledge necessary for survival. In addition, elders knew the patterns of nature and the way to commune with Spirit. However, those values shifted when the frequencies of consciousness shifted. Who needs to "commune with Spirit" when you're busy conquering nations or building empires? The emphasis then became focused on having strength, physical beauty, or the ability to withstand hardship. Later it extended to greater achievements bound up with strength and power—in order for individuals to build platforms of success—whether through financial power, business acumen, or military strength.

In all of this the need to establish one's territory and the power and glory of the Self were the dominant themes. Weakness of any kind was considered anathema. As a result, that further emphasized separation. Now, ask yourself, why would people need to create separation in the first place? There were several reasons. First of all, beneath the absolute pride and power was a fundamental weakness in character and a clear fear that "if I don't keep watch on the top of this mountain, someone will surely supplant me." Compounding that was the absence of true knowledge. To make such arbitrary distinctions among humans was a sign that ignorance reigned.

The Spiritual Path of Aging

Understand that within the Old Paradigm, there is a lack of understanding about the core energetics of human consciousness. What everyone shares in equally is the Soul—and its foundation in Spirit. No one is excluded. When this is missed, unknown, or misunderstood, then any grouping at all is based in separation and illusion. Even your attempt to elevate those of us in Spirit to the level of gods and goddesses, while you remain below as mere mortals and sinners, is part of that Old Paradigm of separation and illusion.

But know that you are on the cusp of a brand new era and a turning point—taking on a powerful new direction. Of course, as you look around, it's easy for you to refute our assertion. That's because whenever a real shift in consciousness is emerging, all the detritus of the old thought forms rises to the surface in protest. So what you have now is a sharp contrast between the old established norms and the new freedom in consciousness. As in any serious revolution, both sides are equally convinced of their rightness, their righteousness, and their superiority. But rest easy. The end of power over or power under is in sight. Remember that it took thousands of years for that consciousness to be cultivated in civilization in the first place.

*This may appear to be a revolution or a civil war. Or we might add, an **un-civil** war—a bloody battlefield between parties! It does represent a huge dueling ground; make no mistake about it. However, the outcome belongs with those who've peeled the illusion from their eyes and have recognized within the depths of their being the fundamental nature of living beings—what everyone shares in common, and **not** what appears to be your differences.*

But the real shift that's coming is not so much a battle as a strategic withdrawal from the battlefield. It is a retreat that leaves fight or struggle far behind. Although it is not an easy *transition, in the long run it is leading you into a more thoughtful, kind and harmonious direction, with the guiding notion that if all beings are equal, then all beings need to be **treated** equally. This is what is meant by an evolution in consciousness. You no longer subscribe to outdated beliefs. You see the underlying pattern of reality and welcome that into your consciousness. We applaud you for any and all efforts within this transition; consider it to be a sacred time for all. We are working with you in this effort, which marks a true evolution from lower vibration and lower frequencies to higher vibration and higher consciousness for the species as a whole. That includes all of you within the aging category; so as of this moment, consider yourselves as an elite gathering of **Enlightened Elders!***

Chapter Fifteen

What About Resilience?

I am grateful that Martha, one of the participants in our Spiritual Path of Aging course, brought up this question in our very last session: "What about resilience?" Although I thought we were moving toward it with our focus on mindfulness, I realized we had spent more time on "letting go" and not enough time on bouncing back!

Merriam-Webster's defines *resilience* as the ability to bounce or spring back into shape. It adds another definition, which is the ability to recover strength, spirit, good humor, and buoyancy. And then the dictionary adds in the word *quickly*—almost as an afterthought. What that immediately brings up is the image of a rubber band. Think of it stretching as far as you can stretch it to wrap around something you want to put in the freezer. If you've stretched it too far, it will break. Then it's no good for anything. If it stretches the right amount, it can keep your container covered—so much the better. But when you carefully unwrap the container and release the rubber band—now it springs back to its original size. So your rubber band is ready to be used again.

Martha pointed out to me that it doesn't actually spring back to its original size. It gets a bit stretched out, and in fact so do we. Though we may not revert to our original size after being stretched or pushed about, we are definitely altered in some way. The fibers and molecules of our being are reshaped and strengthened if we have developed the ability to confront, cope, and process the challenges

What About Resilience?

we've met up with and come out the other side! Then we're clearly on our way to resilience.

That brings to mind another member of our Spiritual Path of Aging group, Mary. To me she epitomizes the picture of resilience in the years that I've known her. In fact, I aspire to be just like her when I hit my eighty-seventh year as she has. Mary has beautiful bright hazel eyes that light up her face when she's smiling; you might never know that she lost her dear husband eight years ago and just a few months back lost her only daughter, who was fifty-six. All that remains of her family now is her son and son-in-law. Her son-in-law lives close by but may be returning to the Cape where he once lived with his wife (Mary's daughter). So dear Mary is now minus husband, daughter (possibly son-in-law), and even her son is a little too far away to be a steady source of comfort.

And yet Mary shines brightly, approaching us with a hug or words of encouragement or a smile. She is the poster child for resilience; oops, I should say the poster *lady*. The question is—how does she do it? Mary sings in the church choir and has been active on various church boards and the Prayer Shawl Ministry. She walks her sweet little dog and takes yoga classes; she does prayer vigils and reads inspiring material. She talks to friends near and far away, and she also sings with the Berkshire Lyric group, which, as of this writing, will be performing Brahms' requiem at Tanglewood shortly. So the long and short of it is that Mary remains fully engaged in all aspects of life—physical, mental, emotional, and beyond. This doesn't mean she hasn't grieved these losses; in fact, she continues to do so. This doesn't mean that she has it all worked out or has shifted her focus of attention (especially after the recent loss of her daughter). But what it does mean is that she's got the ability to spring back; she prays and she sings, and if I can influence her at all, she'll also dance a little cha cha with me when the music's on.

So what about resilience? What it includes, above all, is flexibility and the ability to roll with the punches. As a matter of fact, we actually have discussed the ingredients that comprise resilience. It shows up in our willingness to notice all things, to feel all things, and to move through the varieties of grief and emotion that accompany our losses. And through it all we remain centered in the Self. Gradually we create greater spaciousness and acceptance, allowing ourselves to receive help when we need it, and to be on the receiving end of the loving-kindness we so graciously send out to others. In addition, giving or receiving help implies the willingness to seek knowledge from different sources, as well as being willing to "stop action" (or withdraw from busyness), and to rely deeply on prayer, introspection, and support from friends and family. The process is not "one and done." We draw on these same resources to face the next challenge.

Meanwhile, we continue finding new ways to invest in joyous or creative activities, possibly invoking the "Tell a New Story" game designing a new life and new connections to help us thrive. I love the brief quote from Jeffrey Cranor that my editor Bhavani sent to me: "Death is only the end if you think the story is about you." This is evidence of one more crucial ingredient in resilience—which is having a good sense of humor. I have heard it said that when we cry, our tears are evidence of a great emotional release and letting go; however, when we laugh or poke fun at ourselves, our laughter is evidence of an even deeper integration and acceptance of all that we've experienced.

Chapter Sixteen

A Cause for Celebration?

Amid all of these inquiries, abstractions, and reflections on aging and our spiritual momentum, it's helpful to pause for a moment and step out of the frame. After all, we can become too serious when we're constantly focused on where we are, what's missing, or what still needs improving within our consciousness. As with everything in life, too much self-study can be analogous with self-absorption. And too much self-absorption leads us into the quagmire of self-importance—that endless preoccupation with me, myself, and *mine,* to the detriment of all else.

I have long been a fan of Carlos Castaneda's works, and especially one of the last books he wrote called *The Active Side of Infinity.* There he provides a powerful recipe for receiving the gifts at the heart of each connection in our lives. We first reflect on each relationship and the way that it "sits" or occurs for us energetically. Then we "empty out," becoming silent enough to release any hurts or negativity we've experienced. This happens when we penetrate deeply enough to see the underlying fabric of events and how we may have contributed or created them by default. When we have truly grasped the dynamics present in any of our relationships, the freed-up energy moves us back in the direction of freedom, love, and pure joy. The focus is on freeing ourselves from the *cult of me,* as Castaneda puts it:

The Spiritual Path of Aging

When you move beyond Self-importance into the true nature of being, then you receive the irreducible essence, your unbiased love for each person. And you realize at your core that love is always there just as energy is always there that gives life.[49]

The notion of an irreducible essence within each relationship is pure gold, from my point of view. Love is there; it's always there, even after all the turmoil of living seems to have shoved it out of existence. Let's take this a step further and apply this idea to ourselves. For after all, as aging spiritual pilgrims, we have been the revered subjects of our self-study all along. What if we were able to access that deep stillness Castaneda refers to? That would offer us the opportunity to witness the "underlying fabric of events" within our selves. Seeing so clearly would then help release or unblock old patterns of energy until we realize we have truly freed ourselves. As a result, we can come home to that sweet experience of our unbiased love—for ourselves!

That brings us to a different vantage point altogether. In line with the prior suggestion to "Tell a New Story," it's time for us to call out the great new things that are on their way to us. It's time to announce the positive changes we're making along the way. I'll take the first step.

First of all, after that encounter I had with Loneliness, old energies were dispersed or freed up, and I felt greatly relieved. Though I'm often alone, loneliness doesn't weigh quite as heavily on me as it did before, and I can see through the past beliefs that turned it into an issue. Also, I am more productive now when I'm alone. All of this makes me feel more empowered and happy at the same time!

I love this pithy quote that I ran across from the Abraham-Hicks universe teachings online:

---

[49] Castaneda (page 158)

A Cause for Celebration?

A miracle is my normal life causing me to evaluate what I want, and then letting it in. A miracle is a lapse of normally resistant thought.[50]

What a joy when resistance actually falls away! Then I can celebrate the way I work so beautifully with clients or with groups. I am watching miracles occur in people's lives, while at the same time another miracle is taking place—as I gain more clients day-by-day, it's a windfall in terms of abundance!

I celebrate the way magic keeps showing up in my life. More and more I am paying attention to little urges and intuitions, for they are the precursors to extraordinary magic. Like the hot summer day I joked with a supervisor, letting him know I was wearing a bathing suit to work the next day since the air conditioning was on the blink. Then I added mischievously, "You ought to do the same" to which he responded, "Not a chance." (He wasn't too keen on my silly nature.) On leaving work that evening I took a different route home than I usually do, and lo and behold, who came jogging down the street, dressed only in his bathing trunks? My boss, of course. Even he acknowledged this "strange coincidence."

And then there was the time not long ago when I was out walking, and I saw a beautiful white Alaskan Husky standing with his owner across the street. I SO wanted to meet and greet that beautiful dog! In my mind I envisioned him walking beside me and then I let him know how utterly delighted I was to welcome his sweet presence. In the very next instant, I looked down, and there he was! He had crossed the street and walked over to me, as if to say, "Thank you! I wanted to say hello to you as well…"

I love Seth's instructions for us in *The Magical Approach*:

True creativity comes from enjoying the moments, which then fulfill themselves, and a part of the creative process is indeed

---

[50] Hicks (Online Article)

the art of relaxation, the letting go, for that triggers magical activity.[51]

In addition, we need to add in the experience of effortlessness to our projected creations, in effect saying to the universe, "I'm not going to focus on the problems. Bring me the joy along with the solutions!" And so it is.

Now we've rounded the corner into magical activity and magical demonstrations (with or without rabbits in hats). Clearly, it's time for us to celebrate! That means shifting the lens through which we view our lives! It means gravitating more to the magic, the manifestations, and the miraculous way things unfold, if we just delight in our experience. I love how we're encouraged to move in these new directions, when Thoth, speaking from the distinct perspective of the Divine, lets us know how we're perceived in Spirit:

> *We are celebrating that which you are creating and that which you are aligning with in this Now moment. We invite you to bask in the contribution that you are, the Light Being that you are, the Awakened Consciousness that you are, and the Pioneer in spirit you have always been. Take a moment to acknowledge yourself, congratulate you for what you've done so far; give yourself an "inner high five." Acknowledge that all you're up to is about architecting a new evolution in consciousness.*[52]

With such joyous exultation, there's only one thing left to do—and that is party! As Kool and the Gang used to sing, "Let's all celebrate and have a good time!"

---

[51] Roberts, 1995 (page 8)
[52] Danielle Rama Hoffman (See citation page. 41))

Chapter Seventeen

What Is Your Chief Legacy?

I am so grateful that in the elders class I taught at the First Congregational Church, John, one of the men in the group, pointed out that there was a distinction between what you leave for your kids, whether monetary as in an actual inheritance or property, versus what you leave behind for everyone in terms of opportunities and teachings—which he referred to as being a good ancestor—what a unique twist! We all began to focus on what we're leaving behind and how our individual legacies might turn us into good ancestors.

Later on, I began dwelling on the issue of legacy versus being a good ancestor. Many things popped up. For example, I find myself hating to spend too much money, for then when I go, I imagine there won't be anything left for my family members—especially my nieces, nephews, and godchildren. However, I might pay more attention to what I'm leaving them (beyond a large pile of photographs) that provides guidance or support facing any life challenges coming down the pike.

In order to consider our true legacies, we need to create a broader view of our life work and focus of attention. As parents we had an important role in leaving behind a "legacy" for our children in terms of behaviors, attitudes, and ways to be successful in the world as well as happy and fulfilled. But we can take it a step further by giving thought to the legacies we received from our parents.

The Spiritual Path of Aging

I am so grateful my mother taught me how to be a good cook. I also appreciate the fact that she took my sister and me out on public transportation when we were very young and taught us how to negotiate buses, subways, and the elevated trains. What that created was not only my ability to travel from Northeast Philadelphia to Center City for ballet lessons at the age of seven—but also instilled a great love of travel along with a clear sense of independence, finding my way anywhere from here to India or North Africa and back home again.

I am also extremely grateful that my father's sense of humor continues to travel with me long after he's gone. Sometimes I even get into trouble for being silly or telling too many jokes. But pointing out the absurd is clearly my M.O. In fact, I was recently giggling to myself and wishing that Dad were here, because I had just heard a Frank Sinatra song and remembered how much he loved Old Blue Eyes. Dad would have helped me out when I decided to rewrite Sinatra's song: "You Make me Feel so Young" I can almost hear Dad singing in the car: "You make me feel so old; you make me feel like I'm catching a cold." Or "You make me feel so old; your looks are hot but my feet are cold…"

Humor was his legacy to me, whether he intended it that way or not. Still, I have my father to thank for puns, silliness, and singing in the car. And the key to it all is summarized in that phrase, *whether he intended it or not*. Though we may put a great deal of focus into monetary gifts (and there's nothing wrong with including these as part of your legacy), the real gifts are generally more abstract and sustainable long-term because they affect our behaviors and approach to life.

So when you consider the legacies you hope to leave behind, consider first what gifts naturally came to you from your parents or guardians. Then reflect on your work, your career, and the many activities that have been in alignment with your chief mission in life. Then you can be more deliberate in imagining what legacies

What Is Your Chief Legacy?

you'll leave behind. This is a good time to consider that there are both direct gifts and talents you hand down as well as the more subtle influences coming simply from the way you've lived. It is not only your children or heirs who receive vital legacies from you; it's everyone and anyone from your past with whom there's been enduring (and endearing) contact.

Chapter Eighteen

Preparing to Die

Now the doctor is facing you, holding your chart. She has a rather solemn look on her face, as she announces to you and your family, "I am so sorry, but we have done everything we could, and it still hasn't alleviated your condition. There is nothing else we can do." Then she nods at your family members and adds, "Once you're transferred back home, your family will complete the process for setting up hospice care."

So that's the final news! You're at the stage where death is immanent. Or in other circumstances there may have been an accident, a heart attack, or some other troubling diagnosis, but however it came about, it is now clear! Death is here! For some of us it's a terrifying moment; for others it brings great relief—at last I know! I'm finally heading home.

Before that telling moment; however, the issue has to do with final preparations. Will you find a way to move through this transition with grit and grace? And what about your family and friends? At this juncture we join with various religious leaders who can help carry us through these final moments on Earth. More than any other time in our life cycle, our rabbis, imams, and ministers are there as spiritual and religious guides, offering us friendship, support, prayer and ritual to get through this saddening and often perplexing time of our transition. Having sat by the bedside of many dying folks, I know they can be champions in helping us be present for those who mourn us as well as for ourselves, when we mourn the passing of our lives.

Most Christian traditions provide a formal service either in the church sanctuary or by the graveside; infrequently a service may happen at a funeral home. Each of the key religious or ethnic traditions offer some ritual of mourning or of celebration; some even borrow or replicate their sister religions (as with Islam, which sets aside a specific period of time—generally twelve days—for mourning someone, which is similar to the Jewish practice of sitting Shiva for seven days).

Reflections from the Pastor

No matter what rites or routines may be sanctioned by churches, temples, or synagogues in regard to life's ending, it's often more instructive to speak directly with clergy to discover their approach to dying members and their families. This conveys more of the "flavor" or sense of welcome within the setting as well as the potential openness to members' grief or loss.

While Pastor Brent, of the First Congregational Church of Stockbridge, understands his role as helping and guiding congregants through their final transition, he finds more often than not that his chief role turns out to be listening and being fully present. That is what helps to create safe space for folks to move through the phases of their dying process and for families to grieve in whatever way they need to. Naturally he will offer guidance and instruction. But like any great leader, he first takes the time to follow—that is, to sense the real needs that are emerging and that must be addressed.

In all his years of preaching in different churches, Brent realizes (and instructs people) that there's absolutely no *right* way to do it! Everyone grieves differently; everyone has different needs for creating a funeral or send-off. One thing he hopes is changing is the recognition that attending a funeral or visiting a gravesite is no "proof" that everything's over. "We've said goodbye, now let's get on with life." That's a false premise. Grieving has its own timeline, which turns out to be different for every single person. You can't rush the process.

What interested me were the similarities Brent pointed out in the ceremonies for death and marriage—two distinct life experiences. From his perspective, weddings and funerals share more in common than you might expect. They're both grounded in mystery—whether it's the mystery of life lived and what comes next, or the mystery of love and how to sustain it. Brent works with families of the dying to help them see that a funeral or memorial service needs to ground itself in the larger mystery of life and death—and yet at the same time be fashioned in a way that honors the individual who's dying. It's like walking a tightrope; there's sometimes a bit of a wobble, and often a need to create greater balance between both tendencies.

I was surprised to learn that a few years back, one of Brent's elder church members was adamant that he did not want any kind of funeral or service after his death. Instead, he wanted his wife to throw a party! Coming from a simple "churchy" tradition, she was quite perplexed. Following her husband's death, she questioned Brent about how she could possibly honor her husband's wishes. The solution was truly masterful; she created a party for him, just as he had requested, but prior to that, she held a modified service (created on *her* behalf—to honor him). Surprisingly enough, so many folks showed up for the service that they had to steal folding chairs from the party set-up to accommodate the service.

Inevitably Brent aims to create an environment (whether in church or by the graveside) that welcomes everyone—and that makes room in creative ways for everyone to be fully present. At times it may present a challenge if members of the family have different expectations or different values from the one who is dying. Sometimes dying individuals who've been staunch church goers may clash with extended family members who haven't been in church for years and don't feel obligated to have a funeral to say goodbye. Generally, that's the exception and not the rule; however, it can be a bit of a "dance" which Brent's accustomed to. He rises to the occasion by reflecting back to the families the importance of creating ritual—and by extension—to folding in their own meaning about death and finding their way to grieve the individual in a way that has meaning and purpose for them. It turns out to be an important teaching opportunity, a valuable lesson, and one that supports a greater evolution in consciousness for everyone involved.

Brent reflected on a powerful time for someone who was dying who had run out of pain medication at a critical juncture and was no longer able to move around. Surrendering to this difficulty, she decided instead to sit by the window and just watch leaves falling. It was the perfect fall moment for such intense scrutiny; she wound up sitting there for three days straight and later on she exclaimed to him that she literally saw leaves turning color. He marveled at the ease with which she was able to shift her focus (especially in the face of so much pain) as well as her ability to hold something so dear as leaves turning while her days on Earth were dwindling away.

Death turns out to be a great equalizer—a time when false narratives about life fall away. Knowledge of impending death, according to Brent, often brings folks to a place of sober reckoning. Sometimes when he's working with the dying, Brent feels that as much as he helps the dying—they also *help* him. What he means by that is that frequently the person has arrived at a deeper understanding and in some ways—even a sense of relief—when they know they're actually dying. Since he has supported many people through their transitions, Brent observes how little despair they seem to feel in contrast to their greater appreciation for the moments left, along with an openness to the mystery that awaits them, and a kind of magnanimity toward all who surround them. Often his guidance leans toward honoring the different facets of loss within the grieving process, whether it's the dying person grieving their own loss of life or the family members surrounding that individual. Whatever occurs is what needs to occur and everyone is encouraged to fully *abide* in and acknowledge all the vicissitudes of the death and dying experience.

Reflections from the Rabbi

Speaking with Rabbi Neil Hirsch at his synagogue nestled in a beautiful tree-lined street in Great Barrington was a great joy. In many ways, he was the personification of the very friendliness and companionship suggested by the name of his temple, which is *Hevreh,* or friend in English.

Rabbi Hirsch spoke about the covenantal relationship of the Jewish community which is at the heart of any work with elders or with the dying: "If our key covenant is to be in relationship with God, then everything flows from that; we're committed to caring for one another and providing the kind of support that promotes each one's connection to God."

He then went on to describe the three *mitzvot,* or obligations that must be carried out when someone is seriously ill and heading toward their inevitable end. The first obligation is called *bikor cholim* in Hebrew, which means visiting the sick; the second obligation is referred to as *kavod ha-met,* which consists in giving honor to the person who is dying, and finally the third obligation, *nechum aveilim,* is giving comfort to the mourners. Although these may be called "obligations," Rabbi Hirsch does not consider his work as some kind of social work, where he's doing an intake, or providing a service. Rather he sees it in the light of the original covenant he spoke of, having to do with the instinct to be of help, to companion those in transition, and to share the love of God along with love for one another.

There are two ways relationships within the Jewish community unfold as a result of that original covenant—either through ethical commands, such as love the stranger, or take care of the widowed or the poor. The second is through ritual commands, such as keeping kosher or keeping the Sabbath. The three mitzvot evolve from those commands, and the rabbi's task is to help guide both the dying person and their family members through the various stages at life's end. When death is immanent, he offers the dying person the opportunity to participate in the *vidui,* or prayer of confession; if the person is unable to speak or is unconscious, then it can be said on their behalf. He notes that the key prayer spoken upon awakening and going to sleep, the *Sh'ma*— "Hear O Israel, the Lord our God, the Lord is One"— should be the last words the person recites (or hears upon dying).

Once the person has died, Rabbi Hirsch outlines the phases of ceremony, grieving, and transitioning back to "normal life" that occur for family members. In Judaism, there is always an attempt to bury the person between twenty-four to forty-eight hours after dying, so things happen quickly. For this reason he always counsels families to make final plans for the elderly well ahead of time. He calls this the "gift they give to their future selves," that takes pressure off of last-minute plans and the need to pull everything together quickly, once someone has died. Thus, the funeral happens very soon in this timeframe. In working with families, Rabbi Hirsch observes their need for guidance and support. Their understanding is not that keen on what needs to happen, and he often hears them saying, "Just tell me what to do." Yet, there's wisdom in having done the hardest part first (the funeral) because it's so cathartic. Each step after that helps everyone spiral back from that liminal space—that immersion in grief. The funeral itself is "out of time"; it does not occur in what we might consider "normal time." In fact, the whole structure of time is turned upside down, because the family is then expected to gather and sit shiva for seven days.

"Shiva" is derived from the word sheva, which means seven, signifying the seven days of mourning. When a loved one dies, the Jewish community gathers at the mourner's home to observe shiva. As part of that, *minyanim,* or evening services are held that enable the mourners to recite the Mourner's Kaddish. Often, it is clergy who lead the services, but not always.

At the end of the seven-day period, it is customary to take a walk around the block, to signal that the family has come back into the flow of normal time. The full thirty-day period, known as shloshim, provides a time for spiraling back to some semblance of "normal life," though it's still recognized as a profound period of mourning. The completion of these stages only occurs when a full year is up, and then each succeeding year the person mourned is honored through prayers, recognition, and the lighting of candles on the anniversary of their death.

As with many religious traditions, there is often a good bit of variation even within the framework of Judaism; however, Rabbi Hirsch is both creative and expansive in choosing how to translate the Torah into modern practice. Every day there are new decisions to be made, and he looks to the original covenant—of furthering one's relationship with God—to determine his next steps.

Chapter Nineteen

A "Green" Departure

I am indebted to Reverend Quinn Caldwell, pastor of Plymouth Congregational Church in Syracuse, New York for the two articles that follow, reprinted with his permission from the StillSpeaking Devotional publications. There's something very powerful and (excuse the expression) down-to-earth about Quinn's reflections that upon reading them, I knew I wanted them to be included in this manifesto.

I first met Quinn more than ten years ago when he came to preach at the First Congregational Church in Stockbridge, holding space so that the pastor could travel to Florida with his husband to adopt their sweet baby son. I remember laughing during the service when Quinn assured us that two males were quite capable of caring for a baby (to which he added, "And actually keeping him alive"). He has the kind of humor, coupled with deep devotion that makes me feel very much at home, enjoying his "devious" spirituality. Quinn preached my favorite sermon of all times years ago about moving into a new life experience and starting over again. I have no recollection of the text he used; however, I do remember how memorable the talk was because he gave it while emerging out of the cellar of his home, walking up the steps to come outside and face the camera.

"My Green Funeral" By Reverend Quinn Caldwell[53]

Here is what will happen when I die. I will not go to a funeral home. My partner or my kids will wash and prepare my body. I will not be embalmed. They will wrap me in a linen shroud and lay me out in my living room. If it is high summer, they will lay me on a block of dry ice. They will sit vigil until the time of the funeral.

A minister will perform the funeral within a couple of days, before the recycling bacteria get too much of their work done. Then my people will drive me out into the country, where they will come to the end of the road. From there, they will bear the weight of me on their shoulders as they walk into our local natural cemetery. When we get there, the minister will do the graveside service. Then they will lower me into the ground with ropes... They will sow wildflower seeds over my head, which will, I trust, bloom like crazy as I begin to pay back the molecules I borrowed from the earth all those years ago. Ashes to ashes, dust to dust.

My family will know intimately, with hands and backs and tears, that a death has taken place. They will know that they have done right by the one who died. They will trust in God.

"Green" By Reverend Quinn Caldwell

"But God raised Jesus up, having freed him from death, because it was impossible for him to be held in its power." - Acts 2:24 (NRSV)

On a hill just outside Ithaca, NY, there is a meadow. It looks like a nature preserve: a couple chunky, rustic benches, some wandering paths. If you start walking and look closer, you will

---

[53] Caldwell (page 24)

A "Green" Departure

see here and there large stones in the ground that look native to the site, irregular but carefully flush-mounted. They're carved with names, dates, and epitaphs.

This is Greensprings Natural Cemetery Preserve, one of a growing number of natural burial grounds in the green burial movement. No chemicals are added to bodies to make them last (and leech into the earth around them in the process). No metal or concrete enclosures or boxes. No wood that has been treated, painted, glued, or dyed. Just bodies, natural-fiber shrouds, cardboard cartons, maybe a rough box of native pine if someone felt fancy. Stuff that disappears. No traditional headstones; few even of those flat fieldstones. Wildflowers and native groundcover made of molecules returned from human borrowing seem a better memorial in the eyes of your average Greensprings resident.

Jesus knocked out the door of his tomb; many of us are still planning to be buried in one.

Jesus insisted on being set free; many of us are still planning to one day be put inside boxes inside boxes inside boxes.

Death could not contain Jesus; many of us are still working hard to allow death to entrap our bodies forever.

But on a hill just outside Ithaca, and in places like it all over the world, there's a meadow full of flowers, and trails, and grass, and death slowly being freed back into life.

Prayer

Thank you for the loan of these molecules, God. I promise I'll return them when I'm done. Amen.

Chapter Twenty

Ready to Leave?

Now we move to the fundamental issue we all wind up facing somewhere in the act of living. And that, of course, is the experience of dying, leaving planet Earth for some distant unknown realm. Back in 1973 the eminent author and pastor, Robert E. Neale wrote a compelling treatise on death, called *The Art of Dying*.[54] In this seminal work, he urged the reader to approach death and dying from every possible angle—including what you think or don't allow yourself to think regarding your own death, how you relate to others' passing, plus issues of sudden death, prolonged death, death as a surprise, death as something planned for, and death from suicide. Along with multiple fears—such as the fear of what we're leaving behind versus the unknown that we're headed for, the survey was so extensive, it soon turned into something I considered to be borderline macabre. I felt such angst and anxiety arising during the reading that I realized I'd either have to put the book down or race through to the conclusion without lingering through the remaining chapters.

But I wound up doing neither. Instead, I became fascinated and absorbed by the various quotes and questions, coupled with observations by authors as diverse as Shakespeare, Jung, Rilke, Tolstoy, and Saul Bellow. All along, Neale urged us to make a thorough and well-thought-out inventory of our thoughts, wishes,

---

[54] Neale (*Art of Dying*)

A "Green" Departure

myths, fears, superstitions, hopes, and anxieties regarding our own death, stating that it's pretty much a foregone conclusion we're headed in that direction.

Why is it so hard for us to contemplate our demise? Although it took me a long time (with a great deal of resistance), I finally got around to creating my will and sending copies of it to both my brother and sister in Philadelphia. However, when my brother asked me if it was important for him to read it right away (meaning while I'm still alive), I couldn't bear the thought of him doing it, so I said no. As a matter of fact, I've never opened or read the details of his will or my sister's either. It seems that I just don't want to think about life after my brother, or life after my sister, and finally life after myself. That reminds me of a funny one-liner I read in Neale's book. He alludes to the title of a book that was written by Alexander King. And the title of King's book was simply: *Is There Life After Birth?*

Now that book has been added to my bucket list of things to read in the future. A friend of mine who was very ill and thought he might be on the threshold of death told me he was happy about one thing in particular. I asked what that was, and he said he was finally getting rid of his bucket list. Happily replacing it with all the things he would never get around to doing, he proudly referred to it as his *Fuck-it* List.

One way or the other, we all face the loss of dear friends and family members. For many years my mother was convinced she'd be dead before the year was out. Pretty much every year during our annual Thanksgiving dinner, she warned us that this was it. And since her health had often been precarious, we believed what she said—the first year, the second year, and then the year after that. This may have begun when she was in her late eighties. After quite a number of Thanksgiving dinner warnings, we finally began joking with her about it. Here she was still serving up her scrumptious turkey and side dishes, and another year had gone by. It wasn't until October of 2011, that I finally received a call from my sister, telling me to leave right away for Philly. Mom had died the night before in her sleep. By then, she was ninety-two. Her best friend joked with us, saying we'd all been cheated out of Mom's *dramatic* leave-taking; in fact she got off easy. She simply slipped out one night, and against Dylan Thomas's advice, *went out gentle into that good night.*

Although many of us prefer to keep this matter of death enclosed in a separate silo, Eugene Kennedy reminds us that death and life live side by side:[55]

> *Death is by no means separate from life... We all interact with death every day, tasting it as we might a wine, feeling its keen edge even in trifling losses and disappointments, holding it by the hand, as a dancer might a partner, in every separation.*

Thinking about my own relationship with death and dying, I realize that there were two outstanding moments in my life when I clearly thought I was going to die. The first was just prior to my cardiac catheterization and angioplasty at Bay State Hospital in 2018. Then I had to go back for a repeat angioplasty in the spring of 2022. Besides more shortness of breath and poor health, I was also more depressed the second time around. I remember being plagued by the persistent fear that I would never come out of the surgery—or the hospital—alive. Of course that didn't happen, and I've lived to tell the tale. But nevertheless, something very interesting arose in my awareness from that hospital experience. I realized that I *wanted* to have my life end. And I've never been suicidal in my entire life. But in that moment, I realized that I had crossed the line.

I grasped very deeply that I had passed from being life-focused to being death-focused. It's hard to understand this since most people are very centered in their fully embodied experience and have no

---

[55] Kennedy (From AZquotes online)

A "Green" Departure

bandwidth for death, dying, or exiting the planet. Crossing that so-called line, I felt very open to death, inviting in the opportunity (without actually wishing to do harm or end my life myself). I then knew what it was like to be in touch with one's mortality. Simultaneously, I understood how that same awareness doesn't occur for most life-centric people. At any rate I made my way back again after physical recovery, grasping how a radical shift had taken place in my consciousness.

I realized I was neither *death-denying* nor *death-defying* as Robert E. Neale so eloquently describes in his work, *The Art of Dying*.[56] Instead I might better fit the category of *death-accepting* or *death-allowing,* as Neale calls it. I'm fine to keep living; don't get me wrong. However, I feel more present to the possibility of my own ending—not to cherish or resist—but simply to allow space for it to show up as it must. I am beginning to affirm that we have more power than we admit to ourselves about the design, or the way, in which our death transition occurs. It's not quite the helpless scenario we once thought it might be. And yet, at the same time, the way we proceed with the matter of living in itself tends to predict how we'll move through this matter of dying.

One thing I have learned from talking with a spiritual guide is that when you're ready to make your transition, you need to make a clean break of it. What I gather from that is it means coming to terms with all you have lived—good, bad, or indifferent—and leaving, if not in deep peace and satisfaction, at least with a sense of being full and fulfilled, having done what you truly came here to do. When you have achieved that and can depart without resentments or recriminations, then you slide out of your mortal coil with great ease and effortlessness. If that hasn't been the case, then there's a good bit of back and forth—possible indecision and conflict, which may translate into a nightmarish battle between life

---

[56] Neale (page 6)

and death or staying and leaving. However, since I'm still here, there's no way to prove that. And despite all my conversations, research and obvious immersion in this topic, I must confess that I still have fear about the prospect of dying.

As Henri Nouwen, great Christian priest, writer and teacher, reminds us:

> *Maybe the death you fear is not simply the death at the end of your present life. Maybe the death at the end of your life won't be so fearful if you can die well now. Yes, the real death—the passage from time into eternity, from the transient beauty of this world to the lasting beauty of the next, from darkness into light—has to be made now.*[57]

Again, as we review the new stories that signal our current focus of attention and movement forward, we must also consider if we have "died well to our past…" For that one lengthy death engenders the final short one. I love the image once proclaimed in a channeled session from Emmanuel that experiencing death is like stepping out of a pair of very tight shoes. Ah, if it is that easy—then why so much fear and trembling beforehand?

For me personally, it isn't so much the issue of the death transition itself. I'm actually looking forward to that because I sense it will be an amazing journey into heightened consciousness. The hard part for me is living alone while my family is so far away. Although my worst-case scenario would be dying alone and my body never being found, I am also learning to tell a new story about this. Now I am emphasizing the fact that I am the Creator of my experience—in fact of ALL my experiences, which has to include the way in which I depart from Earth. So although I'm not planning to throw a block party or a festival, I am softening around my dying process and considering it to be a thing of beauty. It's going to be a slow and

---

[57] Nouwen (page 107)

A "Green" Departure

gentle easing out of here, with time for me to acknowledge and say goodbye to all my loved ones.

It amazed me to run across the following quote from the Seth material online—it came almost as if in answer to some of the questions raised about the living and dying process. So, this will help wrap up our inquiry before taking the next steps—i.e., before literally moving on:

> *Some portion of each individual is in direct contact with the very source of its own existence. Your nature is to live and to die. Death is not an affront to life but means its continuation, not only inside the framework of nature as you understand it but in terms of nature's Source. It is, of course, natural then to die.*
>
> *The natural contours of your psyche are quite aware of the inner sweep and flow of your life and its relationship with every other creature alive. Intuitively, each person is born with the knowledge that he or she is not only worthwhile, but fits into the context of the universe in the most precise and beautiful of fashions. The most elegant timing is involved in each individual's birth and death.*[58]

Now, as we prepare for our leave-taking, it's time to conduct an inquiry into your own death with focused concentration and honesty. Consider your response to the following questions: What is your greatest fear about dying? What is your greatest hope? What have you done (or not done) to prepare for your transition? Or do you tend to postpone any thoughts, much like Woody Allen, who said, "I'm not afraid of death, I just don't want to be there when it happens..."[59]

This is a good time to imagine the perfect scenario for your death. What will it look like? How soon would you like to depart? Do you

---

[58] Roberts –Session 821 (Fans of Seth webpage)
[59] Woody Allen Quotes. (n.d.). BrainyQuote.com

want to be alone or with others? What music or prayers might help you make your transition? Is there anything you think might contribute to the feeling of completion—in other words—that you have done everything you wanted to do while here on Earth? And finally, what needs to happen in order for you to welcome in your death?

This is a broad hint to take up this matter as a prelude to the future, and as a ritual that opens you to new creative potential. Remember how much we've alluded to the notion that your thoughts magnetize your reality. Why should death be any different from your lived experience? Perhaps I'll be around to hear your thoughts later on; perhaps I won't. But it's possible we may be able to discuss how things worked out for you when we gather together in the great hereafter. In the meantime, I wish you *Bon Voyage*.

Appendix I: Exercises for the OLD-at-Heart

Below are a number of essay questions and exercises to play with. Although these questions roughly line up with what's been covered in the prior chapters, there's no special order or direction you must take; just browse through and answer the questions that resonate the most for you at this particular stage of life. At any given time, you may want to come back to these questions (or compose your own) to track any changes or evolution in consciousness regarding your Spiritual Path of Aging.

1. Observations on Your Current Aging Process

What changes have you observed in your aging process? What do you most value at this stage of life? What do you regret having to let go of? What has greatly changed or shifted? How can you best take care of yourself amid these changes?

2. On Love, Relationships, and Keeping Your Heart Open

Where is love still thriving or active in your life? Where has love been lost or let go? What helps you keep your heart open? What practices might enhance your love for others or your own self-love? What has love taught you during the course of this lifetime?

3. On Grieving and Loss

In the list of categories included below, circle those where grief is still active and present for you. (Feel free to add other categories that resonate for you.) Then take a few moments to reflect on each loss, and also consider what may help you fully experience and grieve this loss fully.

    (1) Loss of a loved one

    (2) Loss of health, wellness

(3) Loss of home or dwelling

(4) Loss of work or position

(5) Loss of financial stability

(6) Loss of a cherished hope or dream

(7) Loss of faith in oneself

(8) Loss of faith in God

4. Defining Your Spiritual Path

Key Elements or Qualities of a Spiritual Path:

- Aligns with your core values and purpose in life
- Involves the cultivation of wisdom and self-knowledge
- Provides service to the community
- Provides an *inner* sense of fulfillment and joy
- Strengthens your connection to God, Spirit, or a Higher Power
- May involve some type of practice, prayer, ritual, or reflection
- Leads to freedom from suffering or pain
- Becomes a deep expression of compassion and loving-kindness
- Helps to light the way for others on their own path
- Aids in the release of old habits, ineffectual behaviors, or illusions
- Creates the space for deep inner work and transformation
- Offers a sense of lasting happiness and peace of mind
- Leads ultimately to realization (referred to in some circles) as the experience of enlightenment

Considering the various elements of a spiritual path that were outlined in Chapter 1 and are reproduced here—how would you define your spiritual path at this stage of life? What would you say is the key focus? Is there room for service to the community, private prayer or contemplation, or openness to new learning, compassion, or transformation? What practices or new connections might help to further uplift and strengthen your life experience?

5. Awaiting Death and Transition

Before you depart this earthly life, what is yet to be accomplished? What regrets do you have about things left incomplete or undone? What myths about dying can you let go of? What actions will help you feel full and fulfilled, willing, and ready to transition? What support might you create for your final moments?

6. Giving Thought to Your Legacy

Consider the main gifts you received from your parents or guardians? How did their legacy contribute to or help shape your life? Now consider what legacies are you passing on? This has to do with abstract gifts, teachings, or ways of living you modeled in the past, as well as the more tangible gifts of property, money, or behests to charities.

7. Deciding What to Celebrate Now

At this point in time, as you complete this inquiry on your own Spiritual Path of Aging, what are you ready to welcome into your life? Knowing what you now know about your spiritual path, what is waiting to be called into existence? And most importantly, what will you choose to *celebrate* as you pause and congratulate yourself on having completed this powerful sacred journey?

Appendix II: Time for Ritual and Prayer

In this section you will find many suggestions for taking on rituals or prayer to enhance your Spiritual Path of Aging. Depending on your particular religious or spiritual tradition, you may find many of these already quite familiar. Some activities may warrant revisiting or investigating anew. Others may point you in a different direction or serve as a template for entering into an entirely new type of practice. Among the many suggestions, I include the following:

- Keeping a gratitude journal
- Practicing mantra out loud
- Engaging in dialogue to assist with "Fierce Letting Go"
- And of course—silent meditation
- Slow meditative walking in the woods
- The practice of toning or sounding
- Reading or repetition of prayers from different traditions

Keeping A Gratitude Journal

The practice of gratitude is often overshadowed by our concentration on things that are difficult or painful; therefore, it's helpful to create a journal in which appreciation functions as the core reflection. Find a notebook that is artful or beautiful to look at; it may help draw you back into practice. Or feel free to create your very own handmade booklet. Some folks like to leave blank pages to insert drawings or famous quotations. However you set it up, let it become your own private sanctuary in a way—for it's a place you can retire to that helps you remember the grace and joy and beauty hidden within many moments of your life experience.

Practicing Mantra Out Loud

The Spiritual Path of Aging

It is very interesting that repetition of prayers out loud tends to calm and center our minds. And repetition of specific syllables (from multiple traditions) has an even deeper effect, for within the framework of such words and letters is a spark of energy that we resonate with. Thus mantra or prayer repetition ignites a frequency or higher vibration in us that we can recognize as Divine.

Repeating these mantras out loud (or in our own minds, if we stay focused) brings a singular form of concentration and peace that only gets enlarged through time if practiced on a regular basis.

Consider any of these mantras for repetition:

- *Om Shanti Om* (Shanti means peace, so this mantra from the Hindu tradition invokes peace of mind.)
- *Sh'ma Yisrael Adonoy Elohenu, Adonoy Echod.* (Hear, Oh Israel, the Lord our God, the Lord is One.) This mantra from the Jewish tradition brings us back to the essential Unity of our connection with God.
- *Om Gate Gate Paragate Parasamgate Bodhi Svaha*—(from the Tibetan Buddhist tradition: Translated as, Gone, gone, everything is gone to the other shore—to the great Awakening.)
- *Lord Jesus, have mercy on my soul.* (Often repeated many times in succession with additional verses—from the Christian tradition.)
- *Hail, Mary, Full of Grace, the Lord is with thee. Blessed art thou among women, and blessed is the fruit of thy womb, Jesus.* (Also can be repeated at length, from the Christian tradition.)
- *Heenay ma'tov oomanayim shevet achim gamyachad.* (Hebrew song: Behold how good it is for brethren to dwell together in unity.)
- *Om Namah Shivaya*—(Sanskrit mantra: I honor the divine presence within.)

- *Om bhur bhuvaha swaha, Tat savitur varenyam, Bhargo devasya dhimahi, Dhiyo yonaha prachodayat (Gayatri Mantra,* translated as, Oh great Light that gives birth to all consciousness, worthy of our Adoration. Who appears to us through the orbit of the Sun, please illumine our hearts and grant us peace.)

Engaging in Dialogue to assist with "Fierce Letting Go"

Spoken out loud, we usually consider dialogue to be a conversation between two living beings. (Or in prayer between God and ourselves.) However, for the purposes of "Fierce Letting Go," we engage in a different kind of dialogue, which has a therapeutic twist—we speak to whomever or *whatever* it is we need to reconcile with or clear energetically from our fields. Dialogue in this sense is different than ordinary chatter or conversation between people. Here, we are calling upon the fear or blockage and personifying it—allowing it to become an entity that can converse with us. So it might wind up being our fear, our grief, or our conflict; it might also be a real person (whom we're afraid to confront) or someone in our lives who's died, but with whom we still have unfinished business.

In a sense, rather than holding up a mirror that reflects the issue at hand (which is what a therapist is often called upon to do), this dialogue represents a more direct encounter. There is no intermediary or translator of feelings, for in the very act of speaking, self-discovery occurs. That is because taking on the role or mindset of the *other* in itself becomes the mirror reflecting our fears or inhibitions. The "other," after all is invariably the shadow side of ourselves. As a result, this can be a highly creative process, eventually conferring greater freedom and peace, for once we've identified the problem, coming into direct confrontation helps us see more deeply into the core issue, while helping us face old stored up emotions. Invariably the conclusion of such a dialogue leaves us with unexpected relief and release at the same time.

And of Course—Engaging in Silent Meditation

Much has already been said about the practice of meditation. To review the various stages that move from the in-drawing of attention to the deeply absorbed, integrative higher states (known as *Samadhi* in yogic practice), you may wish to revisit Chapter Six. Then as you begin to contemplate your own style of meditation, take into account what it is that deters most people from practice—and that is the distracting quality of their own thoughts. If you subscribe to that argument, then meditation will never take hold as a real practice. What's important to understand is that the mind is never actually free of thought. It's just the speed and frequency that changes. But often when we aspire to meditation, we imagine it will lead us to the cessation of all thought. If only! However, if you can be content to sit and observe the flow of thought, rather than judging the flow of thought or trying to stop it altogether, then you will be well on your way to incorporating meditation as part of your spiritual practice.

I may be repeating myself, but in truth, I can't say it enough—It is terribly important to STOP everything and move into an internal focus. Call it stillness; call it meditation; call it reflection; call it turning off your cell phone; call it sitting by the fire; call it inner silence—it doesn't matter what you call it! What matters is that you actually call it, and then call *on* it, pressing whatever pause button needs to be pressed. Then you have achieved that wonderful space of quiet where you can receive its bountiful calming effect on body, mind and spirit. There is no substitute!

"There have been thousands upon thousands of people who have practiced meditation and obtained its fruits. Don't doubt its possibilities because of the simplicity of its method. If you can't find the truth right where you are, where else do you think you will find it? Life is short. No one knows what the next moment will bring. Cultivate your mind while you still have the opportunity. You will

soon discover the treasure of wisdom, which in turn you can share abundantly with others, bringing them happiness and peace."[60]

Slow Meditative Walking in the Woods

For the most part, this practice is self-explanatory. The walking-in-the-woods part, that is. Most of us are usually walking in a hurry, using locomotion principally to get from one place to another. This is true whether we're walking from our car to place of work or from the bottom of the trailhead to the summit of the mountain. Walking as spiritual practice, however, is unlike any other type of movement. What it requires is a different focus altogether—and that is more internally based. As we're walking, we're not so concerned with getting somewhere or arriving somewhere—but instead on what is happening in that moment—observing the *movements* of our mind, emotions, and our physical being as we take step after step. Of course, we need to watch where we're going to avoid injury, but otherwise the process leads us to the crossroads between nature and our internal environment, allowing us to witness the subtle shifts and changes occurring through such slow movement and focused attention. Insights and *aha's* may arise spontaneously. It can be a beautiful time for centering and grounding ourselves; in fact, walking through a labyrinth laid out with stones in the earth may be one of the most powerful incentives to dive into focused meditation and calm that there is.

The Practice of Toning or Sounding

Nowadays we have become highly sensitized to the effect of different sounds on our minds and bodies. Through the use of binaural beats in music, for example, we can help a client reproduce the corresponding state desired, whether they opt for beta, alpha, theta, or delta frequencies to calm their minds. And there's also the practice of Sound Healing, which, through the use of drums, rattles,

---

[60] From the teachings of HH the Dalai Lama (page 121)

or Tibetan bowls produces different states of repose through the varying qualities of sound.

Many healers agree, however, that one of the most effective meditative practices is to dive in, listen, and receive the qualities of healing inherent in the sound of your own voice. This occurs through the combined effects of slow breathing and the simple, deep but often-monotonous sounds that toning produces. You can do this with mouth open or closed. Work first with your lips firmly pressed together and simply hum, using the sound of "mmm" (as if you were enjoying a fine piece of chocolate). Now change the register. Go as low as your voice can hum and then try the highest key. There is no tune to follow; you're not trying to reproduce a particular melody or song. As a matter of fact, you're not trying to mimic *anything,* other than the deep tones you can access within your voice's own range.

You can then vary the sounds produced by using different syllables, such as *Om*, or *Ah*, or *Ooh*, or *Ee*. In fact many of these line up with the same frequency or vibration of the energy centers in your body. Part of the yogic system, these are known as *chakras*, and when you change the tone or the syllable, you will resonate with the dominant frequency of any of the seven key energy centers in your body. But you don't need to create a science out of this endeavor. Simply apply the art of toning and you will receive great benefit.

Once you feel comfortable listening to the sound of your own voice, you will find that you can sit for longer periods, for the sounds produced will engage your mind and senses, drawing you into a calm and more internalized focus. A simple and effective way to move more deeply into meditation, you will find toning a great adjunct to other spiritual practices that you're exploring.

Consider Prayers from Different Traditions

> *No matter what country you were born in, the soul of it is prayer. Every one of your churches and temples; every one of*

A "Green" Departure

your holy places consists of prayers. In fact, prayers offered in earnest are the most miraculous tools. Traveling through life, I came very close to death five times; however, I survived by the grace of God. To pass through difficulties was like passing through a great fire. The tool that brought me safely through each time was prayer.[61]

Thus in every culture, in every religion and in every tradition, some form of prayer is present and engaged in, whether singly or in groups or congregations. There is a beautiful process of *entrainment* that occurs when we enter into prayer states—and it helps us resonate to higher energies, feel deeply connected to one another, to our inner being, and of course to the Divine.

Prayer is an expression of gratitude, of love, and of relationship. It helps you to center yourself and gives nourishment to the soul. It recognizes your divine connection, reconnects you with your own holiness, and nurtures your relationship with Spirit...Prayer serves as a passageway out of the concrete mind and into the realm of possibilities.[62]

Prayers are often divided into different categories, such as prayers of confession, forgiveness, or prayers offering others loving-kindness, or requesting healing. Whatever the basic format, prayers are invariably our attempt to connect with Spirit and ask for deeper help and guidance. In the following section, a number of prayers are offered for everyone's benefit and for further reflection; however, the most effective of all may be the prayers we ourselves create arising from our own lives and the deepest wishes of our hearts. After reading through these variations from different traditions listed below, choose a prayer or two that resonate with you and spend time absorbing both its meaning and its energetic impact as you recite it out loud or to yourself.

---

[61] Levitt, 2004 (page 130)
[62] Engels-Smith (page 35)

An Islamic Prayer for Peace

In the name of Allah, the beneficent, the merciful: Praise be to the Lord of the Universe who has created us and made us into tribes and nations that we may know each other, not that we may despise each other. If the enemy inclines towards peace, do thou also incline towards peace, and trust in God, for the Lord is one that hears and knows all things. And the servants of God Most Gracious are those who walk on Earth in humility, and when we address them, we say, "Peace."

(United Nations' Day of Prayer for World Peace)

The Lord's Prayer

Our God, who art in Heaven, hallowed be Thy name. Thy kingdom come; thy will be done, on Earth as it is in heaven. Give us this day our daily bread, and forgive us our trespasses, as we forgive those who trespass against us. Lead us not into temptation but deliver us from evil, for Thine is the kingdom, the power, and the glory, forever and ever. Amen

(Chief prayer of Christianity—adapted from Matthew's Gospel 6:12)

Foundational Jewish Prayer

Thou shalt love the Lord thy God with all thy heart, with all thy soul and with all thy Might. And these words, which I command thee this day shall be upon thy heart. Thou shalt teach them diligently unto thy children. Thou shalt speak of them when thou sittest in thy house, when thou walkest by the way, when thou liest down and when thou risest up.

(Adapted from Deuteronomy Chapter 6).

A "Green" Departure

The Jabez Prayer

Oh that You would bless me indeed, and enlarge my territory—that Your hand would be with me, and that You would keep me from evil, that I may not cause pain.

(Christian prayer, adapted from 1 Chronicles 4:10)

Ancient Sanskrit prayer

Lead us from the unreal to the real/ Lead us from darkness to light, and Lead us

from death to immortality.

(Often considered one of the oldest recorded prayers on Earth.)

Iroquois Prayer of Gratitude

We give thanks to our mother, the earth, which sustains us.

We give thanks to the rivers and streams, which supply us with waters.

We give thanks to all herbs, which furnish medicine for the cure of our diseases.

We give thanks to the corn, and to her sisters, the beans and squashes, which give us life.

We give thanks to the wind, which moves the air and banishes diseases.

We give thanks to the moon and stars, which give us their light when the sun was gone.

We give thanks to the sun, which has looked upon the earth with a beneficent eye.

The Spiritual Path of Aging

Lastly, we give thanks to the Great Spirit, in whom is embodied all goodness, and who directs all things for the good of earth's children.[63]

An English Translation of the Aramaic Lord's Prayer, adapted

O Cosmic Birther of all radiance and vibration! You create all that moves in light. Soften the ground of our being and carve us a space within us where Your Presence can abide. Fill us with Your creativity so that we may be empowered to bear the fruit of Your mission. Let each of our actions bear fruit in accordance with your desire. Endow us with the wisdom to produce and share what each being needs to grow and flourish. Untie the tangled threads of destiny that bind us, As we release others from the entanglement of past mistakes. Let us not be seduced by that which diverts us from our true Purpose, but illuminate the opportunities of this present moment, for You are the ground and the fruitful vision, the birth-power and fulfillment, as all is gathered and made whole once again. Amen.[64]

"Aging Metta," by Lewis Richmond (A Prayer of Loving-Kindness for Old Folks)

"As I grow older, may I be kind to myself; As I grow older, may I accept joy and sorrow; As I grow older, may I be happy and at peace."[65]

Mourner's Kaddish—Jewish Prayer for those Mourning the Dead

Yitbarach v'yishtabah, v'yitpa'ar v'yitromam, v'yitnasei v'yithadar, v'yit'aleh v'yit'halal sh'mei d'kudsha, b'rich hu, l'ela min kol birchata v'shirata, tushb'hata v'nehemata, da-amiran

---

[63] Energy Magazine (page 36)
[64] Aramaic Prayer (From Snopes Online)
[65] Richmond (*Aging* book, page 209)

A "Green" Departure

b'alma, v'imru amen. Y'hei sh'lama raba min sh'maya, v'hayim, aleinu v'al koi yisrael, v'imru amen.

"Let his great name be blessed forever and to all eternity. Blessed, praised and glorified, exalted and extolled and honoured, magnified and lauded be the name of the Holy One, blessed be he; though he be high above all the blessings and hymns, praises and consolations which are uttered in the world; and say ye, Amen."

Sufi Prayer

Now is the time to know that all that you do is sacred.

Now, why not consider a lasting truce with yourself and God?

Now is the time to understand that all your ideas of right and wrong

Were just a child's training wheels to be laid aside,

When you can finally live with veracity and love. ...

This is the time for you to deeply compute the impossibility that

There is anything but Grace. Now is the season to know that

Everything you do is sacred.[66]

---

[66] Ladinsky, ed. (page 160)

Acknowledgments

Although it only took me eight weeks to write this book, in truth I've been in the process of assembling this material my entire life. That's because the spiritual teachings set forth here have been accumulating from all my various travels and traditions, teachers and touchstones along the way. So please bear with me as we move through this final offering. You might only need two hours to read through the entire work; however, I would leave more than that to wander through this final section of acknowledgments. That's because in large part, it encompasses the key teachers, friends, religious and spiritual mentors who've been my traveling companions all along this aging path of spirit and grace.

First of all, I wish to heartily thank my initial group of *guinea pigs*—the elders from the First Congregational Church of Stockbridge, who were willing to engage in ten weeks of dialogue and investigation into this broad topic: the Spiritual Path of Aging. And for allowing us space to explore this topic (as well as being the incredible religious preacher and teacher that he is), I offer deep gratitude and thanks to the church's pastor—Pastor Brent Damrow.

So many brilliant teachers—so much divine wisdom to impart! I am indebted to Danielle Rama Hoffman, who's led me on amazing spiritual journeys from here to Southern France and on out to the *galaxies*. She is the teacher, Guide, and developer of Divine Transmissions, and the one who channels Thoth, the Magdalenes, and the Council of Light. Much of the material in this work (along with the understandings supporting it) is due to her benevolent wisdom and support.

I am also blessed in knowing Reverend Quinn Caldwell and Rabbi Neil Hirsch, who've contributed important perspectives along with

Pastor Brent to broaden the reach of this work. And so many others have either deliberately or inadvertently contributed to the development of these chapters! It would take pages and pages to list everyone, but at least I can acknowledge the incredible contribution of channeled material from Jane Roberts (channeling an entity called Seth) and Esther and Jerry Hicks (channeling an entity called Abraham), as well as the beautiful assorted teachings of Cynthia Bourgeault, Thomas Merton, St. John of the Cross, Joseph Goldstein, Jack Kornfield, Pema Chodron, and Jon Kabat-Zinn. Thanks also to Carlos Castaneda and Victor Sanchez, who helped me understand the Toltec path of Recapitulation.

I would be remiss if I didn't mention the amazing work of the HeartMath Institute out in Boulder Creek, California—which has contributed deeply to my understanding of stress, peace, and the ability to generate states of true *coherence*. Likewise, I am profoundly grateful to Janet Mentgen's instruction; she passed on the amazing secrets of energy healing to me in her work as the originator of Healing Touch.

And so many different ideas and understandings, rituals, and spiritual practices came about through my exposure to different faith traditions and different teachings. I am forever indebted to Yogi Ramiah, Rabbi Harold Waintrup, Patrice Fields, Paramahansa Yogananda, Amrit Desai, Swami Kripalu, His Holiness the Dalai Lama, Thich Nhat Hanh, Henri Nouwen, and Lewis Richmond. In addition, I can't help but praise the works of Rilke, Rumi, Hafiz, and Gay and Kathlyn Hendricks—who've explored and *exploded* amazing knowledge and teachings on love onto the scene. And finally I thank all the unknown authors who've brought texts and scriptures to us to deepen our faith and understanding of spirit, including the Holy Bible, the I Ching, the Bhagavad Gita, the Koran, and the Upanishads. Thank you, thank you—all of you—you've been amazing guides and teachers for me.

A "Green" Departure

And there is one admittedly weird acknowledgment I must make—and that is offering my thanks to the town of Stockbridge, Massachusetts. I am grateful that you turned me down when I applied for a job as chair of your Council of Aging. In the short run, it hurt a lot because I knew in my heart that I was the best candidate for the job. But in the long run, it freed me up to write this book—which of course was a blessing. All that I put into this book's outline was actually part of my original proposal to you to work with the seniors in this community. Too bad—you missed out.

Thanks to Michelle Vandepas and my sweet tribe at GracePoint Publishing, who clearly saw this as a decent offering and had the courage (and good sense) to take me up on the offer. And thanks to my sweet goddaughter Erika Wainwright—marketing maven and perfectly pleasing publicist. Thanks go to Bhavani Lorraine Nelson as well; she's not only an extraordinary editor but also has the voice of an angel!

Thank you, thank you—everyone! You're all incredible lifesavers and powerful soothsayers, celebrating the intersection between growing old and traveling a sparkly spiritual path—I am so grateful to know you all and to have you as my Divine Traveling Companions! All I can say is Hallelujah!

Bibliography

Scott Berinato, Senior Editor, *That Discomfort You're Feeling is Grief,* Harvard Business Review, https://hbr.org/2020/03/that-discomfort-youre-feeling-is-grief March 23, 2020.

Sister Bhakti, *Building our Relationships on a Spiritual Foundation,* Online Speech, from the Self-Realization Fellowship, https://www.you tube.com/watch?v=AFo10vfew-4 2023.

Franz Borkenau, *The Concept of Death,* as quoted in Death and Identity, ed. by Robert Fulton, John Wiley and Sons, 1965, New York, New York

Cynthia Bourgeault, *Mystical Hope,* Cowley Publications, Cambridge, 2001.

William Bridges, Ph.D., *Making Sense of Life's Transitions,* Addison-Wesley Publishing Company, Reading, Massachusetts, 1980.

Reverend Quinn Caldwell, "Green," Article in *Before You Die,* StillSpeaking Publications, 2022.

Reverend Quinn Caldwell, "My Green Funeral," article in *Before You Die, Reflections & Resources,* StillSpeaking Writer's Group, Cleveland, Ohio, October 24, 2022.

Carlos Castaneda, *The Active Side of Infinity,* Harper Collins, New York, 1998.

Pema Chödrön's Six Kinds of Loneliness, in Lion's Roar, May 15, 2023, c/o website: https://www.lionsroar.com/six-kinds-of-loneliness/

Richard B. Clarke, translator, *Hsin-hsin Ming: Verses on the Faith-Mind*, By Seng-ts'an, Third Chinese Patriarch, Online article, pp. 1-13, October 9, 2008, http://www.mendosa.com/way.html

Megan Devine, *It's OK that you're NOT OK,* Sounds True, Boulder, CO, 2017

Do Creative People Live Longer? --Online article excerpted from The Journal of Aging and Health, October 14, 2020. https://www.worldlifeexpectancy.com/do-creative-people-live-longer

Engels-Smith, *Prayer,* quoted in Energy Magazine, Nov/December 2015

English translation of Aramaic Lord's Prayer: https://www.snopes.com/fact-check/lords-prayer-aramaic-english/

Katharine Esty, Ph.D., *EightySomethings: A Practical Guide to Letting Go, Aging Well and Finding Unexpected Happiness,* 2019, Skyhorse Publishing, New York, New York.

Focus on Healthy Aging, Monthly Newsletter, produced by Icahn School of Medicine at Mount Sinai Hospital, New York, New York. (Belvoir Media Group, Norwalk, CT), Issue FH-23D-D1DFHSC

Joseph Goldstein, *Insight Meditation: The Practice of Freedom,* Shambhala Dragon Editions, Boston, 1993.

Joseph Goldstein, *Mindfulness: A Practical Guide to Awakening,* Shambhala Press, Poston, 1970

Thich Nhat Hanh, *The Diamond that Cuts through Illusion,* Shambhala Press, Boston, 2007.

Thich Nhat Hanh, *How to Love,* Penguin-Random House, New York, 2014.

Esther Hicks (channeling Abraham's teachings online): *Abraham-Hicks Universe,* https://www.facebook.com/groups/478477180

Bibliography

8207584/?multi_permalinks=9699330623418320&notif_id=1685019677453970&notif_t=group_highlights&ref=notif\

Patrick L. Hill and Nicholas A. Turiano, *Purpose in Life as a predictor of Mortality across Adulthood,* in Psychological Science, July 2014. https://www.canyonranch.com/wellstated/post/permission-to-grieve/

B.K.S. Iyengar, *Light on Yoga,* Schocken Books, New York, 1979, pages 45-52

Jon Kabat-Zinn, *Mindfulness for Beginners*, Sounds True, Boulder, Colorado, 2016.

Eugene Kennedy. AZQuotes.com. Retrieved May 29, 2023, from AZQuotes.com Web site: https://www.azquotes.com/author/20073

Soren Kierkegaard, Online Quote: https://www.azquotes.com/author/8000-Soren_Kierkegaard/tag/reality

Hansol Kim and Hyun Kang, *Ageism and Psychological Well-Being Among Older Adults: A Systematic Review,* in the Journal of American Society on Aging, Fall, 2005, PP 87-90, *https://pubmed.ncbi.nlm.nih.gov/35434202/*

Jack Kornfield, *A Path with Heart,* Bantam Books, New York, 1993

Daniel Ladinsky, translator, *The Gift: Poems by Hafiz, the Great Sufi Master*, Penguin Compass, New York, 1999.

His Holiness the Dalai Lama, *Dzogchen*: *Heart Essence of the Great Perfection*, Snow Lion Publications, New York, 2004.

Jo Ann Levitt, *Mindfulness: The Art of Witnessing Experience,* Article written for Kripalu Center Personal growth programs, 1998.

Jo Ann Levitt, Ed, *Pilgrim of Love: The Life and Teachings of Swami Kripalu*, Monkfish Book Publishing, Rhinebeck, New York, 2004.

Fleet Maull, Ph.D., *Neuro-Somatic Mindfulness, A Direct Path to Awakening,* 2022, Online E-book and Seminar, Heartmind.co

Dr. Gladys McGary, The Well-Lived Life, c/o https://gladys mcgarey.com/

Megret et al, *Research Studies on Ageism*, Review of Research published online, c/o https://www.ncbi.nim.hih.gov/pmc/articles/PMC5550624

Thomas Merton, *The Inner Experience: Notes on Contemplation*, HarperCollins, New York, 2003

Colin Milner, Online Interview with Dr. Stephanie Ludwig, *Death by Design*, Journal of Active Aging, 2022, https://www.icaa.cc

Stephen Mitchell, editor, *The Enlightened Mind: An Anthology of Sacred Prose*, HarperPerennial, New York, 1993.

Robert E. Neale, *The Art of Dying,* Harper and Row Publishers, New York, 1973.

Henri J.M. Nouwen, *The Inner Voice of Love*, Doubleday, New York, 1996.

Lewis Richmond, *Aging as a Spiritual Practice: A Contemplative Guide to Growing Older and Wiser,* Gotham Books, New York, 2012

Lewis Richmond, *5 Spiritual Practices for Aging Well*, Huffington Post article, February, 2012. 5 Spiritual Practices for Aging Well | HuffPost Religion

Jane Roberts, *The Magical Approach,* Amber-Allen Publishing, California, 1995

Jane Roberts, *The Nature of Personal Reality*, Amber-Allen Publishing, California, 1994

Bibliography

Jane Roberts,—(Articles, quotations, and updates on Jane Robert's combined volumes of channeled Seth material)- found on *Fans of Seth Material website*: https://www.facebook.com/groups/8461791483/?multi_permalinks=10161113741321484%2C10161112025566484%2C10161114942261484%2C10161113517271484%2C10161112686001484&notif_id=1685622230176720&notif_t=group_highlights&ref=notif

Fr. Richard Rohr, Getting Back to our First Nature: Why the Mind is the Key, Online article posted November 20, 2013, https://www.huffpost.com/entry/getting-back-to-our-first_b_4298903

Nicki Scully, *Sekhmet: Transformation in the Belly of the Goddess*, Bear & Company, Vermont, 2017

Martin Seligman, Marie Forgeard and Scott Barry Kaufman, *Creativity and Aging: What We can Make with What we Have Left,* Online article posted March 21, 2016, https://scottbarrykaufman.com/wp-content/uploads/2016/05/Seligman-Forgeard-Kaufman-2016.pdz

Melinda Smith, Lawrence Robinson, and Jeanne Segal, *Coping with Grief and Loss,* Online article, https://www.helpguide.org/articles/grief/ coping-with-grief-and-loss.html Posted January 10, 2023.

Spirituality and Aging: A Guide for Seniors on Faith, Meaning, and Connection, Online article from GreatSeniorLiving.com. Posted April 20, 2020 https://www.greatseniorliving.com/articles/spirituality

Laura Roe Stevens, *Permission to Grieve,* Online Article posted December 15, 2002.

Ten Signs that you've crossed Over to the Old Category: Article online c/o https://www.msn.com/en-us/lifestyle/parenting/10-signs-that-you-ve-crossed-over-to-the-old-category-and-

young-people-are-judging-you/ss-AA1bW1Pu?ocid=entne
wsntp&pc=U531&cvid=7fb74055de5f4a2396dc06881bec86d
4&ei=49

Eckhart Tolle, as quoted from his work, *The Basic Delusion,*
https://www.awakin.org/v2/read/view.php?tid=446

United Church of Christ Website: https://www.uccresources.com/collections/banners-posters

Alberto Villoldo, Online Quote: https://www.awakening-intuition.com/alberto-villoldo-quotes.html

Robert L. Weber & Carol Orsborn, *The Spirituality of Age: A Seeker's Guide to Growing Older*, Park Street Press, Rochester, New York, 2015.

Additional Resources

Jo Ann Levitt

Jo Ann provides Healing Touch and Counseling services and guides monthly online Meditation classes. She is available for private consultations, keynote talks, personal retreats, and workshops, both in person and online. To learn about her books and services, consult her website: www.joannlevitt.com

The following of her works are also available on Amazon:

Awakening to the Power of Source: Your Guide to Co-Creating with the Divine, Scribes of Light, an Imprint of GracePoint Publishing, Colorado Springs, CO, 2021.

Channeling the Sacred: Activating your connection to Source, Scribes of Light, an Imprint of GracePoint Publishing, Colorado Springs, CO, 2020.

The Twenty-first Century Gospel of Jesus Christ, as told to Jo Ann Levitt, Xlibris, 2019.

Pilgrim of Love, Monkfish Book Publishers, New York, 2004. (Biography and teachings of Swami Kripalu, edited by Levitt).

Sibling Revelry: 8 Steps to Successful Adult Sibling Relationships, (with sister and brother, Marjory and Joel Levitt), c/o Dell Publications, New York, 2001.

Danielle Rama Hoffman

Danielle is an international coach and channel, keeper of the Ascended Master Lineage of Thoth, leader of the New Paradigm of Unity Consciousness, and successful entrepreneur since the early

'90's. She leads programs in person and online along with tours of sacred sites in France and ancient temples in Egypt. You can learn more about her mentoring and assorted products and programs, including her latest masterful production of *Magdalene Manifestation cards* on her website listed above. She also holds an imprint with GracePoint Publishing called *Scribes of Light*.

To access Danielle Rama Hoffman's collected works channeling Thoth and the Council of Light, go to her website, www.DanielleramaHoffman.com or check for these works on Amazon or wherever books are sold:

The Temples of Light, by Danielle Rama Hoffman, Bear and Co. Press, VT, 2009.

The Council of Light, by Danielle Rama Hoffman, Bear and Co. Press, VT 2013

The Tablets of Light, by Danielle Rama Hoffman, Bear and Co. Press, VT, 2017

About the Author

Besides being a trained personal growth and meditation teacher, Jo Ann Levitt has a diverse background in nursing, Healing Touch, and working as a Spiritual Guide. She continues to offer transformative group and individual experiences and owes this volume in particular to a 10-week course in the Spiritual Path of Aging, which she offered at the First Congregational Church of Stockbridge.

A prolific author, lecturer, and energy worker, Jo Ann was a senior Kripalu faculty member for thirty years as well as a behavioral therapist, Healing Touch practitioner and Spiritual Wellness Guide at Canyon Ranch in the Berkshires. Through her years of channeled writing, teaching and counseling, Jo Ann recognizes the need for each of us to partner with Spirit in order to bring forth works that are a match to our life purpose and serve the highest good.

For more great books from Scribes of Light Press
Visit Books.GracePointPublishing.com

If you enjoyed reading *The Spiritual Path of Aging*, and purchased it through an online retailer, please return to the site and write a review to help others find the book.

www.ingramcontent.com/pod-product-compliance
Lightning Source LLC
Chambersburg PA
CBHW022106040426
42451CB00007B/144